CLIMATE CHANGE

The Science Behind Melting Glaciers and Warming Oceans

with Hands-On Science Activities

Joshua Sneideman
and Erin Twamley
Illustrated by Alexis Cornell

Titles in the **Build It Yourself Accessible Science** Set

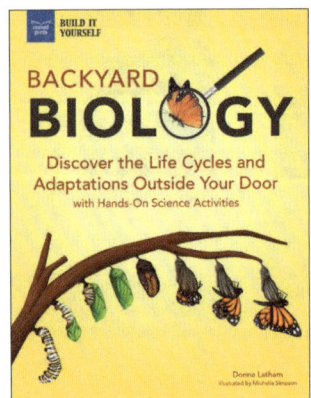 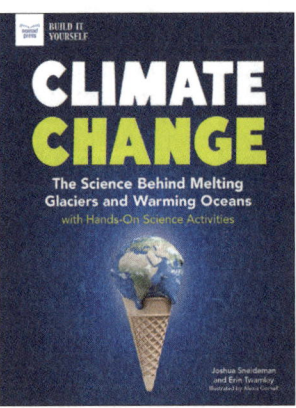  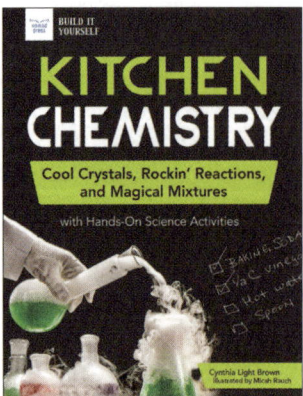

Check out more titles at www.nomadpress.net

In memory of my loving father, Harvey Sneideman.
Joshua Sneideman

For Ella and Noah, may you live in a green world where science and all living things thrive.
Erin Twamley

Nomad Press
A division of Nomad Communications
10 9 8 7 6 5 4 3 2 1
Copyright © 2020 by Nomad Press. All rights reserved.

No part of this book may be reproduced in any form without permission in writing from the publisher, except by a reviewer who may quote brief passages in a review or **for limited educational use**. The trademark "Nomad Press" and the Nomad Press logo are trademarks of Nomad Communications, Inc.

This book was manufactured by Versa Press, East Peoria, Illinois
April 2020, Job #J19-12323
ISBN Softcover: 978-1-61930-899-2
ISBN Hardcover: 978-1-61930-896-1

Educational Consultant, Marla Conn

Questions regarding the ordering of this book should be addressed to
Nomad Press
2456 Christian St., White River Junction, VT 05001
www.nomadpress.net

Printed in the United States.

CONTENTS

Timeline. . . iv

Introduction
Welcome to Spaceship Earth . . . 1

Chapter 1
Goldilocks and the Three Planets . . . 10

Chapter 2
Source of Life: the Sun . . . 24

Chapter 3
The Power of
Greenhouse Gases . . . 42

Chapter 4
Examine an Ancient Climate . . . 56

Chapter 5
Earth Has a Fever . . . 74

Chapter 6
Decide the Future of Planet Earth . . . 90

**Glossary • Metric Conversions
Resources • Essential Questions • Index**

Interested in Primary Sources? Look for this icon.

Use a smartphone or tablet app to scan the QR code and explore more! Photos are also primary sources because a photograph takes a picture at the moment something happens. You can find a list of URLs on the Resources page. If the QR code doesn't work, try searching the internet with the Keyword Prompts to find other helpful sources.

🔎 climate change

TIMELINE

2000 BCE: The Chinese first use coal as an energy source.

1754: Joseph Black discovers carbon dioxide.

1774: Joseph Priestley discovers oxygen.

1781: The stagecoach is the worldwide standard for passenger travel.

1800: Homes consume most of America's energy.

1856: The first scientific paper on climate change is published by Eunice Foote.

1858: The first successful oil well in North America is established in Oil Springs, Ontario, Canada.

1882: The first hydroelectric dam is built by Thomas Edison near Niagara Falls in New York.

1883: The first solar cell is developed.

1890: The mass production of automobiles begins, creating a larger demand for gasoline.

1958: Scientists begin collecting data for carbon dioxide levels in our atmosphere in Mauna Loa, Hawaii.

1958: Scientists publicly state that rising carbon dioxide levels from factories and automobiles are causing the atmosphere to warm, which is melting the polar ice caps and leading sea levels to rise.

1970: The first Earth Day is held in the United States on April 22.

TIMELINE

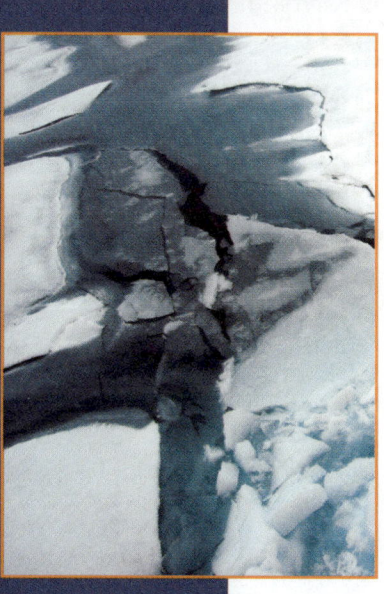

1970: The Environmental Protection Agency (EPA) is created to implement federal laws that protect the environment.

1979: The first solar panels are installed on the White House.

1991: The first offshore wind farm is built in Europe.

1992: The Energy Star label is introduced to identify energy-efficient appliances.

2013: Nearly 21.7 percent of electricity generated worldwide comes from noncarbon sources.

2016: Carbon dioxide measurements in the atmosphere pass 400 parts per million (ppm) for the first time in human history.

2017: In reaction to President Donald Trump's decision to withdraw the United States from the Paris Agreement on climate, more than 3,800 leaders from businesses, local governments, schools, and more pledge to continue climate action.

2018: Swedish teenager Greta Thunberg first goes on a school strike to protest lack of government action on the climate crisis. Her movement eventually goes global and includes 1 million strikers.

2019: The world's population reaches 7.7 billion.

2019: Solar energy systems are located on more than 5,000 K–12 schools in the United States.

August 2019: Iceland holds the first funeral for a glacier lost due to climate change.

Introduction

WELCOME TO
SPACESHIP EARTH

Imagine our planet as a spaceship orbiting the sun in space. Just as a spaceship carries everything astronauts need to survive and thrive, our Spaceship Earth provides us with all the necessities for life on our planet. Welcome aboard Spaceship Earth!

When you watch a spaceship take off or look at photos of life inside a spacecraft, it's easy to see that the spaceship's passengers have to carry everything they need with them, including enough food, water, and fuel to last the entire flight. There are no grocery stores or gas stations in space! The ship also has to have systems to control both the temperature and the quality of the air, which have to be just right for the astronauts to survive.

ESSENTIAL QUESTION
Why is it important to track data for long periods of time instead of short periods of time?

CLIMATE CHANGE

WORDS TO KNOW

environment: everything in nature, living and nonliving, including plants, animals, soil, rocks, and water.

climate: the average weather conditions of a region during a long period of time. These conditions include temperature, air pressure, humidity, precipitation, winds, sunshine, and cloudiness.

habitable: capable of supporting life.

climate change: a change in global climate patterns. In the twentieth century and beyond, climate change refers to the dramatic warming of the planet caused by increased levels of carbon dioxide in the atmosphere primarily resulting from human activity.

fossil fuels: a source of energy that comes from plants and animals that lived millions of years ago. These include coal, oil, and natural gas.

migration: the movement of a large group of animals, such as birds, due to changes in the environment.

natural resource: a material or substance such as gold, wood, and water that occurs in nature and is valuable to humans.

carbon dioxide (CO_2): a combination of carbon and oxygen that is formed by the burning of fossil fuels, the rotting of plants and animals, and the breathing out of animals or humans.

atmosphere: the mixture of gases surrounding a planet.

By thinking of Earth as a spaceship, you can begin to see how important it is to have fresh water to drink and clean air to breathe. There's absolutely nowhere else we can find these essential things.

Our **environment** and our **climate** keep our home **habitable**. Whether you live in hot, dry New Mexico or cool, rainy Oregon, you depend on the earth's systems to control the climate's delicate balance.

Most of the earth's systems are powered by the sun. The wind and water cycles bring rain that refills our freshwater sources while recycling the earth's fresh air supply.

When large changes occur to the earth's systems, our planet may experience CLIMATE CHANGE. Climate change is the WORLDWIDE shift in the earth's WEATHER PATTERNS in response to burning FOSSIL FUELS.

Have you noticed different weather patterns where you live? Have you heard in the news that storms are stronger and more frequent than they used to be? We experience climate change in many forms, from shorter winters and longer summers to changes in rainfall patterns and animal **migration** routes.

All of the earth's inhabitants have to adapt to the impact of climate change. Many scientists and citizens are working together to find solutions to the problems of our changing planet.

WELCOME TO SPACESHIP EARTH

TAKE CARE OF SPACESHIP EARTH

There are almost 8 billion people living on this planet. Each one uses **natural resources** every day. We chop down trees for wood to build houses and burn for warmth. We use water to drink and bathe and wash dishes. We dig up gold and other metals to make jewelry, cars, and cell phones.

We also eat meat, produced from the more than 1.5 billion cows, 2 billion pigs, and 22 billion chickens on Earth! Each pound of meat requires hundreds of pounds of water and food and produces many pounds of waste. That means our meat and dairy consumption impact our planet. In fact, some scientists believe that eating meat is worse for the environment than driving a car.

That's not to say driving a car isn't also bad for the climate! Transportation accounts for much of the **carbon dioxide (CO_2)** that ends up in our **atmosphere**.

The Blue Marble is a famous photograph of the earth taken on December 7, 1972, by the crew of the *Apollo 17* spacecraft.

CLIMATE CHANGE

WORDS TO KNOW

nonrenewable: resources that we can't make more of and that can be used up.

greenhouse gas: a gas such as water vapor, carbon dioxide, or methane that traps heat in the atmosphere and contributes to climate change.

oxygen: a gas in the air that people and animals need to breathe to stay alive and which is the most plentiful element on the earth.

livestock: animals raised for food and other uses.

Many forms of transportation use the burning of fossil fuels as an energy source. When you fill up your car with gas at the gas station, you're pumping a product made from fossil fuels.

Think about your daily life. Do you get driven to school? Do you take a bus to an afterschool program? Do your parents drive to work? Where does the food on your table come from and how does it get to your house? How did your new sneakers get from where they were made to the store you bought them from to your closet?

Most of the transportation around the world uses fossil fuels. You or someone you know might have an electric car that uses a rechargeable battery, but these environmentally friendlier types of transportation are still rare. We have to come up with new types of transportation that use a type of power that does not contribute to climate change.

The production of beef contributes to climate change.

WELCOME TO SPACESHIP EARTH

Eunice Foote

Eunice Foote (1819–1888) was the first scientist to make the connection between the amount of carbon dioxide in our atmosphere and climate change. As early as 1856, she submitted her data to the American Association for the Advancement of Science, but because she was a woman, she was not allowed to join the organization or present her findings. A man had to present them for her. Her work laid the foundation for other important scientists, including Charles David Keeling (1928–2005), to measure the carbon dioxide levels in our atmosphere. From Foote's initial work to today, we have been able to track carbon dioxide levels and discover that the amount in our atmosphere is rapidly increasing.

The more people on the planet, the more resources we use. But many of these resources are **nonrenewable** and will eventually run out. That is why it is very important we use our resources wisely. Our individual choices have an impact on the entire world.

In 1862, **CARBON DIOXIDE** was discovered to be a **greenhouse gas**, which traps **HEAT** in our atmosphere and contributes to climate change.

MEASURING CHANGE

One thing that is greatly impacted by human behavior is the atmosphere. Many gases, including nitrogen, **oxygen**, and carbon dioxide (CO_2), make up our atmosphere. The levels of these gases must remain balanced in order for our atmosphere to support life. Changes to our atmosphere can have enormous, life-altering consequences for all life on earth.

CO_2 is a gas that traps heat. Human activities are the primary cause of the majority of the increase in CO_2 levels in our atmosphere. Using fossil fuels in our cars and factories and burning forests to make room for more **livestock** are ways humans release CO_2 into the atmosphere. Our increased levels of CO_2 are contributing to global climate change.

CLIMATE CHANGE

WORDS TO KNOW

data: facts and observations about something.

water vapor: the gas form of water.

species: a group of living things that are closely related and can produce young.

Scientists at the Mauna Loa Observatory in Hawaii have been monitoring CO_2 levels there since 1958. The graph of measurements gathered on CO_2 levels at the Mauna Loa Observatory is known as the Keeling curve.

The Keeling curve is named after American scientist Charles David Keeling, who discovered a way to measure CO_2 in the atmosphere. As you can see from the graph, CO_2 levels rise every year. In fact, we are reaching levels not seen in the last 3,000,000 years.

Scientists study climate change by making observations, gathering **data** through scientific inquiry, and thinking creatively and critically about different theories. What impact do humans have on the environment? What happens when we damage it? How does this affect our climate? Scientists ask these questions, the same ones that we will look at in this book.

Take a look at the graph showing rising CO_2 levels in this video. What could this mean for the future?

Scripps Oceanography Keeling 2019

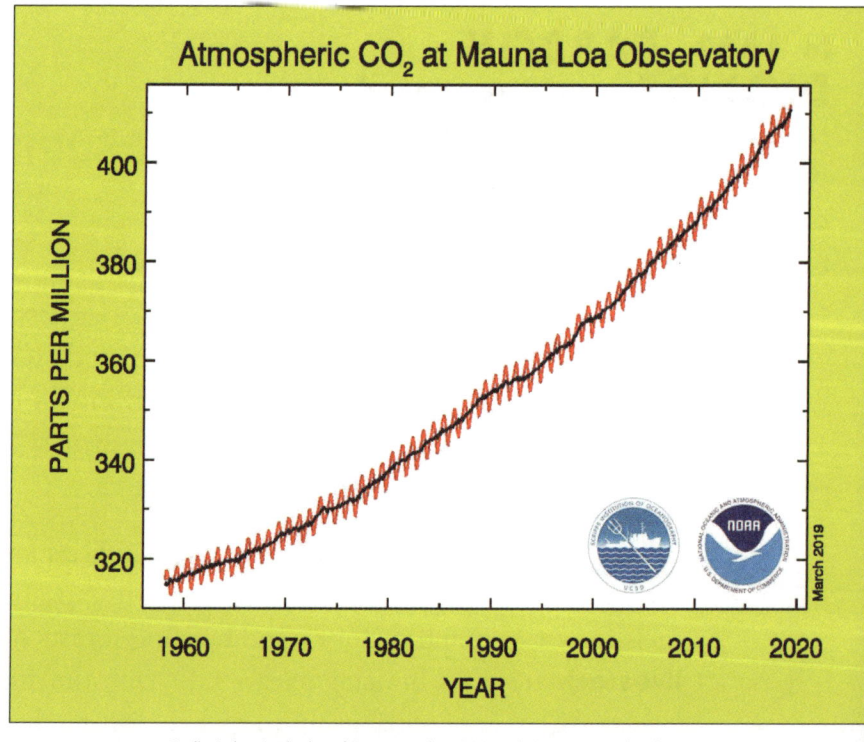

Credit: Scripps Institution of Oceanography NOAA Earth System Research Laboratory

WELCOME TO SPACESHIP EARTH

The Mauna Loa Observatory today
Credit: Christopher Michel (CC BY 2.0)

Why is it important to ask these questions and explore the science behind the answers? Just as a spacecraft needs maintenance and requires that its occupants live a certain way, so does Spaceship Earth. If we want to continue to thrive on this planet, we need to change the way we do things, the way we eat, and the way we live.

We need to find solutions to the problems that are causing the climate of Earth to change in ways that are irreversible. It's important not only so the human **species** will survive, but because millions of other species depend on the health of this planet, too.

For thousands of years, people thought of air as a single substance. They didn't know it was actually a MIXTURE of gases. Air is a mixture of NITROGEN, OXYGEN, ARGON, CARBON DIOXIDE, WATER VAPOR, and more.

CLIMATE CHANGE

In *Climate Change*, we'll take a closer look at the relationships between the atmosphere, the ocean, the land, and Earth's inhabitants to discover how they've changed and why. We'll also be proactive in thinking about the future and what we can do as individuals to help keep the planet healthy.

We need to take care of Earth, just as we'd take care of a spaceship, so that it can take care of us!

Good Science Practices

Every good scientist keeps a science journal!

Scientists use the scientific method to keep their experiments organized. Choose a notebook to use as your science journal. As you read through this book and do the activities, keep track of your observations and record each step in a scientific method worksheet, like the one shown here.

Question: What are we trying to find out? What problem are we trying to solve?

Research: What is already known about the problem?

Hypothesis/Prediction: What do we think the answer will be?

Equipment: What supplies are we using?

Method: What procedure are we following?

Results: What happened? Why?

Each chapter of this book begins with an essential question to help guide your exploration of climate change. Keep the question in your mind as you read the chapter. At the end of each chapter, use your science journal to record your thoughts and answers.

ESSENTIAL QUESTION

Why is it important to track data for long periods of time instead of short periods of time?

INVESTIGATE
WEATHER

How are weather and climate similar to a man walking a dog? **Find out in this video!**

🔎 man dog weather climate

How is **weather** different from climate? Weather can be described as day-to-day conditions. From a bright, sunny day to a snowy day, weather can change quickly. Climate, on the other hand, is long-term weather patterns across many years. Let's explore some of the characteristics of weather.

▶ **Think of three characteristics of weather** that might influence temperature, such as **humidity**, clouds, and wind. Read or watch the 7-day forecast from a few different sources.

▶ **In your science journal, make your own predictions for the next seven days.** Be sure to predict for the same hour of each day.

▶ **Collect data on the weather for one week** at the same time of day for the same location. Use a data table similar to the one below to record your predictions and data.

Date	Prediction	Temperature	Characteristics of weather		

▶ **What did you learn about the weather?** How did your predictions compare to your data? Were the 7-day forecasts correct? Why do forecasters often get the weather wrong?

Try This!

Have a friend in a different region of the world track weather data at their home. Is their weather more or less predictable than the weather where you are? Do different regions have different variability in their weather?

WORDS TO KNOW

weather: the temperature, rain, and wind conditions of an area, which change daily.

humidity: the amount of moisture in the air.

Chapter 1

GOLDILOCKS AND THE
THREE PLANETS

To understand climate change, we really need to understand our planet. And to understand the planet, it's helpful to look at other planets in our **solar system**. Why do we live here and not, say, on Mars or Venus? What's different and similar about the planets around us? Could conditions be right for life on other planets?

ESSENTIAL QUESTION

How do scientists know if a planet is a Goldilocks planet? What do they measure to find out?

Remember the story of Goldilocks and the three bears? A little girl named Goldilocks sneaks into the bears' home and tries to find food that's not too hot and not too cold, a chair that's not too big and not too small, and a bed that's not too hard and not too soft. She is looking for things that are just right.

GOLDILOCKS AND THE THREE PLANETS

Scientists who study planets can relate to the story of Goldilocks as they explore the universe with powerful tools. They are looking for places where life might exist—where conditions are just right.

A GOLDILOCKS PLANET

Planetary scientists examine whether a planet is too hot or too cold, too big or too small, and whether the atmosphere is too thin or too thick for life to exist. They are hoping to find planets where conditions are just right for liquid water. Planetary scientists call these planets "**Goldilocks planets**."

Earth is a Goldilocks planet. Its conditions—including the atmosphere—are just right for water to exist as a solid, liquid, and gas. Think about all the water on Earth. From frozen glaciers in the Arctic to flowing oceans, all the way up to the clouds and moisture in the air, water on Earth is everywhere.

WORDS TO KNOW

solar system: the collection of eight planets, their moons, and other celestial bodies that orbit the sun.

planetary scientist: a person who studies the planets and natural satellites of the solar system.

Goldilocks planet: a planet that orbits in the habitable zone around a star.

orbit: the path of an object circling another object in space.

rotation: a turn all the way around.

elliptical: oval or egg-shaped.

ASTRONAUTS have described **EARTH** as the **BLUE PLANET**. Images from space show that nearly **71 PERCENT** of the planet is covered by **BODIES OF WATER**.

Johannes Kepler

How do we know about the **orbits** of planets? We can credit planetary scientists, including Johannes Kepler (1571–1630), who have observed planets and their **rotations** through telescopes. Before Kepler proved otherwise, people thought planets orbited the sun in perfect circles, but Kepler discovered that the orbits of planets are **elliptical**. NASA named the space telescope used to search for planets after Kepler. The Kepler Space Telescope has discovered more than 1,000 planets since it was first launched in 2009.

CLIMATE CHANGE

WORDS TO KNOW

habitable zone: the region at a distance from a star where liquid water is likely to exist.

gravity: a force that pulls objects toward each other and all objects to the earth.

extremophile: an organism that can survive in environments that most others cannot.

organism: a living thing, such as a plant or animal.

A planet's distance from the sun is another key characteristic of a Goldilocks planet. Goldilocks planets cannot be too close to the sun or too far from the sun. If a planet orbits too closely to its sun, it will be too hot for life to exist. If the planet's orbit is too far away, it will be too cold. The area where an orbit is just right is called the **habitable zone**. A planet in the habitable zone won't be too hot or too cold—it will be just right.

Our atmosphere makes Earth a habitable place. Planets that are too small, such as Mars, don't have enough **gravity** to maintain an atmosphere. They cool too quickly for life to exist. A planet that is too big, such as Jupiter, is made of mostly gas and ice.

12

Extreme Living

Extremophiles are small **organisms** that can live in some of the most extreme conditions. They live where most humans cannot go. Extremophiles can be found in the super-heated waters of the ocean floor near heat vents, in the extreme saltiness of the Dead Sea, in the freezing cold of Antarctica, and even in the driest deserts on the planet. They provide us with clues that life may be possible in some of the most unexpected places—maybe even on the super-heated surface of Venus!

HOT TIMES ON VENUS

To understand why Earth is a Goldilocks planet, let's look more closely at planets that aren't supportive of life.

Get up before daylight or stay out after sunset and you can often see Venus in the sky. Venus is the brightest object in the night sky, after the moon. It looks like a bright, yellowish star. Venus is the second-closest planet to the sun, after Mercury, and the hottest planet in our solar system. How hot is Venus? Even metal will melt on this planet!

Take a look at a video made from data from NASA's *Magellan* spacecraft.

🔍 NASA Venus video

Some people think Venus is extremely hot because it's close to the sun, but the real reason Venus is so hot is its super-thick atmosphere. Venus is covered in clouds so thick that almost no heat escapes back to space. The heat-trapping gas CO_2 makes up 96 percent of Venus's atmosphere. It is so hot that all the water on Venus exists only as water vapor. We can see how Venus's atmosphere works by observing a phenomenon here on Earth. In a parking lot!

The moon has no ATMOSPHERE to trap heat from the sun, so the moon is one of the hottest places in the solar system during the day and one of the coldest at night.

CLIMATE CHANGE

WORDS TO KNOW

wavelength: the distance from crest to crest in a series of waves.

infrared: an invisible type of light with a longer wavelength than visible light, which can also be felt as heat.

greenhouse effect: a process through which energy from the sun is trapped by a planet's atmosphere, warming it.

methane: a greenhouse gas composed of carbon and hydrogen that is colorless and odorless.

Have you ever gotten into a car that has been parked in the sun on a summer day? What's it like inside? Hot!

Sunlight enters through the glass windows and heats up the materials in the car, such as the seats and dashboard. Heat can't pass through the glass as easily as light because it vibrates at a different **wavelength**. The heat's waves are **infrared**. The air inside the car gets hotter and hotter, and when you open the door several hours after leaving it, you encounter very high heat!

Venus is like the car. Light gets in and heats the surface of the planet, and then the heat can't get back out again. The heat has nowhere to go because the atmosphere on Venus, similar to the glass windows of a car, won't allow the heat to escape. The CO_2 in Venus's atmosphere prevents the heat from leaving the planet. This is known as the **greenhouse effect**.

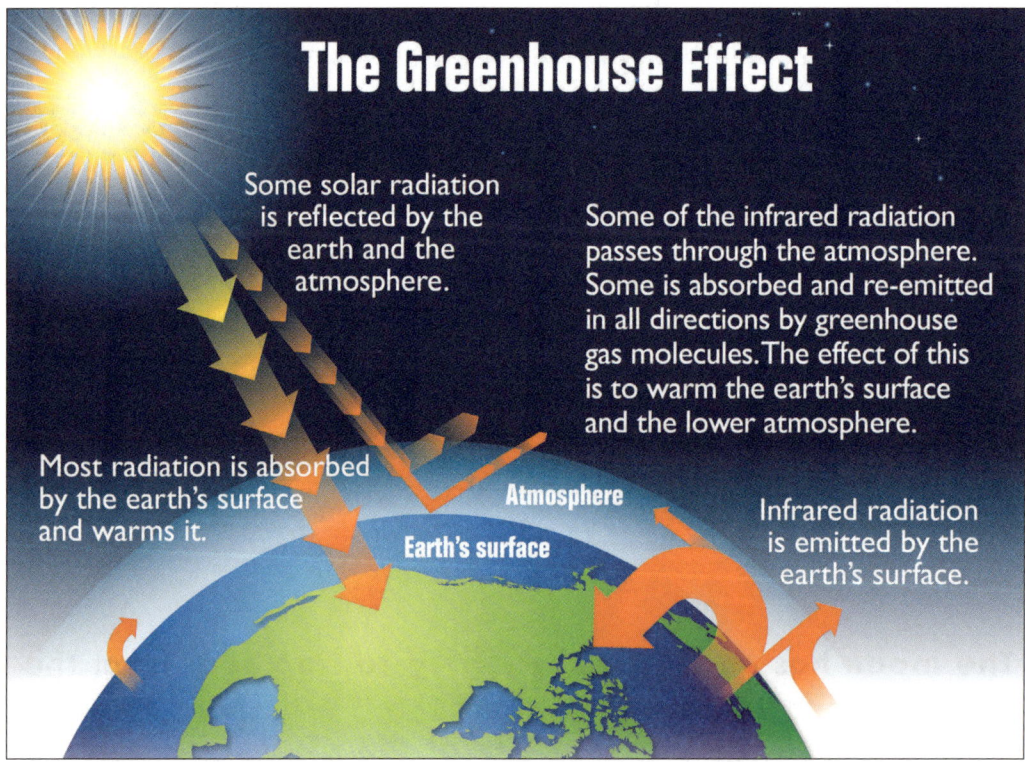

GOLDILOCKS AND THE THREE PLANETS

Here on Earth, we are experiencing a similar effect. As the amount of greenhouse gases increase in Earth's atmosphere, more heat gets trapped within the atmosphere and absorbed by the air, land, and ocean, causing the temperature of the planet to rise. This contributes to Earth's changing climate. Why do you think this is?

Carl Sagan

Planetary scientist Carl Sagan (1934–1996) was the first scientist to correctly explain the mystery of the high temperatures of Venus as a massive greenhouse effect. Sagan fell in love with astronomy as a child when he learned that every star in the night sky was a distant sun. He helped NASA's *Apollo 11* astronauts before their flights to the moon, and helped design NASA's Mariner, Viking, Voyager, and Galileo missions.

Greenhouse gases exist on our Earth naturally. Carbon dioxide, **methane**, and water vapor help to regulate the temperature on Earth and are important for our water cycle. But the amount of greenhouse gases on Earth must be kept just right. Human activity, such as burning fossil fuels, is increasing the amount of these greenhouse gases, creating a growing change in the climate.

Scientists describe the extreme temperature of Venus as a "runaway greenhouse effect." This means the atmosphere heats up to such a high degree that it never cools down again.

Is Venus a Goldilocks planet? The super-hot temperatures and thick clouds on Venus make it hard for scientists to study its surface. The planet remains little explored and hidden in mystery. In 1982, an unmanned Russian spacecraft landed on Venus and sent some beautiful color images back to Earth. About two hours after landing on the surface, the spacecraft was destroyed by the extreme heat.

CLIMATE CHANGE

WORDS TO KNOW

engineer: a person who uses science, math, and creativity to design and build things.

collaborate: to work together with other people.

COLD TIMES ON MARS

Scientists know more about Mars—which is sometimes called the red planet because of its reddish color—than they do about Venus. In fact, scientists know more about the surface of Mars than we do about the floors of our very own oceans! Scientists use telescopes and rovers, which are car-sized, remote-controlled space exploration vehicles, to collect data and take pictures on Mars's surface.

The atmosphere of Mars is very thin, and this is part of the reason we know so much about this planet. It allows us to clearly see its surface.

Controlling the Rover

The rovers on Mars are controlled by people here on Earth. Colette Lohr is an **engineer** and strategic mission officer and Dr. Vandi Verma is a space roboticist—they work together to operate the Mars rover *Curiosity*. Dr. Verma co-wrote and developed the computer programs that tell *Curiosity* what to do! Commands are sent via satellite and usually take about 20 minutes to reach *Curiosity*. Operating *Curiosity* is a big job, taking nearly 90 people a day to make sure it doesn't break down. Lohr established Women's Curiosity Day on June 26, 2014, to highlight the role of women in science. On this day, women took over almost all the rover support jobs. Why is it important to **collaborate** when exploring outer space?

GOLDILOCKS AND THE THREE PLANETS

The thin atmosphere of the planet also affects the temperature of Mars. Light from the sun enters the atmosphere, bounces off the surface, and leaves, allowing very little time for the planet to warm up.

If Venus is like a car with its windows rolled up, Mars is more like a bicycle. Mars allows all of its heat to escape back into space because the atmosphere is too thin to trap the heat.

NASA has been exploring MARS since its first successful mission to Mars in 1964, when *Mariner 4* took 21 pictures of the SURFACE. Since then, the United States has successfully launched 26 missions to Mars.

Planet	Average Surface Temperature
Mars	-80 degrees Fahrenheit (-62 degrees Celsius)
Earth	57.2 degrees Fahrenheit (14 degrees Celsius)
Venus	864 degrees Fahrenheit (462 degrees Celsius)

CLIMATE CHANGE

> **WORDS TO KNOW**
>
> **element:** a substance whose atoms are all the same. Examples include gold, oxygen, and carbon.
>
> **molecule:** a group of atoms bound together to form a new substance. Examples include carbon dioxide (CO_2), one carbon atom and two oxygen atoms, and water (H_2O), two hydrogen atoms and one oxygen atom. Atoms are the smallest particles of matter.

Did you know that we have discovered different states of water on Mars? Using rovers, rock and clay analysis, and satellites, scientists have confirmed the existence of ice on the surface, water vapor in the atmosphere, and conditions that point to flowing water. A piece of ice as large as California and Texas combined was found on the red planet. The water and ice are incredibly salty, but the existence of flowing water means that Mars is more habitable than we previously thought. Is Mars a Goldilocks planet? Why or why not?

That brings us to Earth. Why does one planet in our solar system have an abundance of life while the others appear to have no life?

Sunlight enters the atmosphere and generates heat, but the right balance of **elements** and **molecules** prevents all that heat from being trapped. Just enough escapes so that liquid water, and life, can exist on Earth. All of these characteristics help create a climate that can support life. Earth has all the right conditions.

> Follow along with NASA's *Opportunity* Mars rover in this video. Why does it take so long for the rover to get from one place to another and to do testing?
>
> 🔍 Opportunity NASA rover video

The *Global Selfie* mosaic was built using more than 36,000 individual photographs drawn from the more than 50,000 images tagged #GlobalSelfie and posted on or around Earth Day, April 22, 2014.

As you'll read in the following chapters, you can do plenty of things to make sure the climate on Earth stays "just right." In the next chapter, we will explore how climate and life are connected to the sun.

> **ESSENTIAL QUESTION**
>
> How do scientists know if a planet is a Goldilocks planet? What do they measure to find out?

CAN CRUSHER

CLIMATE KIT
- ice water
- saucepan
- empty soda can
- oven mitts
- cooking tongs
- science journal and pencil

Is an empty soda can really empty? It might not have any soda in it, but it is full of air. Earth's atmosphere pushes in all directions—it's inside the can pushing out and it's outside the can pushing in. The **air pressure** pushing out is in balance with the air pressure pushing in. What happens if we create a **vacuum** inside the can, making the pressure on the outside greater than the pressure on the inside? Let's find out!

Caution: Have an adult help you with the hot can.

▶ **Fill a saucepan with ice water** and set it aside.

▶ **Pour 1 tablespoon of water into an empty soda can.** Use oven mitts and cooking tongs to heat the can on the stove. Boil the water until a cloud of steam escapes from the opening in the can.

▶ **Quickly flip the can upside down into the ice water saucepan.** What happens? Record your observations in your science journal.

Earth's **AIR PRESSURE** is **135 TIMES** greater than the air pressure on Mars. On Venus, the air pressure is **92 TIMES** greater than that on Earth. What would happen to the empty soda can on the surface of Mars or on the surface of Venus?

Think About It!

Why is compacting **recyclables** and other waste a good idea? What might be different about our world if we never crushed cans or plastic bottles when we threw them away?

WORDS TO KNOW

air pressure: the force of air on something.

vacuum: a space in which there is no air.

recyclable: something that can be recycled by shredding, squashing, pulping, or melting to use the materials to create new products.

EXPLORE THE
PLANETS

CLIMATE KIT
- chalk
- science journal and pencil

Our solar system is part of a big universe with planets, moons, and many galaxies. Understanding the size of our universe is a big job! In this activity, create a map of our solar system with chalk in your driveway or on a sidewalk. Use your science journal to take notes about each planet.

Caution: Ask an adult for permission to draw on a driveway or sidewalk.

▶ **Draw a sketch of the planets in your journal.** Do some research and answer the following questions.

* What planets are closest to the sun?
* What are the biggest planets?
* What color is each planet?

▶ **Decide on a manageable scale.** For example, 1 foot might represent the distance between Earth and the sun.

▶ **Select a different color chalk** to represent each planet.

▶ **Draw the solar system on a sidewalk or driveway.** Be careful of other people around you! Can you fit the solar system using your scale?

Think About It!

Choose one of the planets you drew to do more research on. Does the planet have a solid surface? What do scientists think the atmosphere consists of? Has ice or water been discovered there? Is there any possibility this planet supports life? Using your research, draw a cross-section of this planet to show what might lie under the surface.

Massive!

The solar system is HUGE. What are other objects on Earth that are massive in scale? How would you compare them to yourself? One World Trade Center is 1,776 feet tall. How many times larger than you is that? Can you think of other objects of massive size to compare yourself to?

MAKE A
TELESCOPE

A telescope is a scientific instrument that helps us see faraway objects such as planets and stars. Telescopes use a pair of special lenses. An objective lens collects light from a distant object. An eyepiece lens refocuses the light to allow you to see the object. Telescopes come in various sizes and with different lenses. You can create your own simple refracting telescope to explore the moon.

CLIMATE KIT
- 2 cardboard tubes with one fitting snugly inside the other
- 2 magnifying glass lenses between 1 and 1½ inches in diameter with one larger than the other

▶ **Neatly tape the edges of the smaller magnifying glass lens** to one end of the smaller cardboard tube. This will be your eyepiece.

▶ **Neatly tape your larger lens to the end of the larger cardboard tube.** This is your objective lens, which collects light from the object the telescope is pointed at and beams it to the eyepiece. It magnifies that light enough so your eye can see the object.

▶ **Try out your refracting telescope** by pointing it at a piece of printed paper across the room. Adjust the cardboard tubes with one inside the other to change the focus. Can you make all the writing clear enough to read through your telescope?

▶ **Take your telescope outside at night and look at the moon.** What can you see? With an adult's permission, find a map of the moon online so you can identify the areas you spot through your telescope. Draw your own map of the moon and label all the areas you can see with your telescope.

Try This!

Try finding star clusters in the sky. Research online to discover the names of these stars and keep track of what you see in the nighttime sky in your science journal.

WORDS TO KNOW

lens: a clear, curved piece of glass or plastic that is used in eyeglasses, cameras, and telescopes to make things look clearer or bigger.

objective lens: in a telescope, the lens that collects light from a distant object.

eyepiece lens: in a telescope, the lens that refocuses the light to allow you to see the object.

refracting telescope: a telescope with a lens that gathers light and forms an image of something far away.

BUILD A
SOLAR COOKER

You can use light from the sun to cook food! Construct a solar oven to heat up a piece of pizza or make s'mores. It will work to heat up things, but it won't get hot enough to burn you or bake more complex things such as cookies.

> **CLIMATE KIT**
> ° empty pizza box
> ° aluminum foil
> ° black construction paper
> ° newspaper
> ° clear plastic wrap
> ° something to heat up, such as cold pizza

Caution: Be sure to have an adult help you.

▶ **Make sure the pizza box** is folded into its box shape and closed.

▶ **Trace the outline of a piece of notebook paper** in the center of the box lid.

▶ **Carefully cut along three edges of the rectangle** that you just traced on the lid of the box to form a flap of cardboard. Gently fold the flap back along the uncut edge to make a crease.

> Think about how far the **FOOD YOU EAT** has to travel to get from where it is grown to **YOUR PLATE**. This distance is called **FOOD MILES**. Eating locally produced food **REDUCES** the amount of carbon released into the **ATMOSPHERE**.

▶ **Wrap the inside of this flap with aluminum foil.** Tape it on the outside to hold it firmly. Try to keep the tape from showing on the inside of the flap. The foil will help to reflect the sunlight into the box.

▶ **Open the box and place a piece** of black construction paper on the bottom of the box. This will help your oven absorb the sun's heat.

▶ **Roll up newspaper into 1½-inch-thick rolls.** Fit them around the inside edges of the box and secure with tape. This insulation will help hold in the sun's heat.

▶ **Cut two pieces of plastic wrap 1 inch larger than the flap opening.** Tape one piece of plastic wrap to the underside of the flap, over the foil. After taping one side, be sure to pull the plastic wrap tight, and tape down all four sides so the plastic is sealed against the foil.

Tape plastic wrap here

Tape plastic wrap here

Pizza goes here

❯ **Tape the other piece of plastic wrap over the flap opening.** Again, be sure the plastic wrap is tight and tape down all four edges to form a seal. Why is this important? How is the plastic wrap acting like an atmosphere?

❯ **Place a piece of cold pizza in the box and place the box in the sun.** Open the flap and turn the box so the foil is facing the sun. Move the flap up and down and note how it reflects the sunlight.

❯ **Use a ruler or stick to prop up the flap** so that it bounces the sunlight into the box, right on the pizza. Wait about a half hour for the box to warm up in the sun. Enjoy your warmed-up treat!

Think About It!

Can you use your solar oven if it is cold outside? Place a towel or blanket under the box so the bottom doesn't get cold. Set up the oven in the same way. Did your oven get just as hot as when it was warm outside?

SOURCE OF LIFE: THE SUN

What did you have for breakfast this morning? Eggs and toast? Cereal and orange juice? An apple with peanut butter? Bacon? The sun is responsible for the energy in everything you ate for breakfast. This is because the sun is the primary source of energy in almost every **ecosystem**. That might make sense when you think of the oranges in your orange juice, but bacon?

> **ESSENTIAL QUESTION**
>
> How does the sun affect Earth? Could we have life without the sun?

Think about it—bacon comes from pigs. Pigs eat grass, vegetables, and grain to get the energy they need to grow. The grass, vegetables, and grain can grow only because of the sun. Did you have milk for breakfast? Milk comes from cows, and cows, too, get their energy by eating grass and grain. The sun powers the entire system of life.

SOURCE OF LIFE: THE SUN

Plants use sunlight to make sugar from carbon dioxide and water. This sugar, which is stored in the plant's cells, is the source of energy for almost all **food chains** and **food webs**. Most life, including the pig that produced your bacon and the cow that made your milk, can trace the energy in their food back to the sun. When you bite into an apple, you are tasting the sun!

The sun's light powers most of Earth's systems. The sun gives us light and heat. Without it, Earth would be a cold, dark place that could not support life. Could the apple grow in deep space, where the sun doesn't shine and the temperature is -270 degrees Fahrenheit (-168 degrees Celsius)?

As you learned in Chapter 1, the sun's energy is trapped by gases in the atmosphere. This trapped energy is absorbed by the oceans and the land, all to the effect of warming the planet.

> **WORDS TO KNOW**
>
> **ecosystem:** a community of living and nonliving things and their environment.
>
> **food chain:** a community of animals and plants where each is eaten by another higher up in the chain.
>
> **food web:** a network of connected food chains.

As you eat your delicious breakfast, you have the SUN to thank for the ENERGY it provides your body.

25

CLIMATE CHANGE

WORDS TO KNOW

global warming: an increase in the average temperature of the earth's atmosphere, enough to cause climate change.

renewable energy: a form of energy that doesn't get used up, including the energy of the sun and the wind.

chemosynthesis: the process some organisms use to create energy from chemicals instead of the sun.

mass: the amount of matter in an object.

hydrogen: a colorless gas that is the most abundant gas in the universe.

helium: a light gas often used to fill balloons. It is the most abundant element after hydrogen.

compress: to squeeze a material very tightly.

nuclear fusion: the process of hydrogen converting to helium, which releases energy and light.

Does this mean the sun is causing climate change? NASA scientists and satellites have been studying the sun for decades. Data collected shows that the sun's energy is released in a regular pattern. Since 1950, this pattern has not changed. Planet Earth isn't receiving any more energy from the sun than it did in the past.

But still we know the planet is warming up. The vast majority of scientists and citizens agree that humanity's demand for energy is causing climate change. We need energy for everything, from growing food to making more cell phones. For more than 100 years, we have burned fossil fuels that release greenhouse gases into the atmosphere. The increased greenhouse gases are trapping a greater amount of heat in the atmosphere every year, contributing to **global warming**.

Do we need to burn fossil fuels? Could we instead tap into the power of the sun for the energy we need?

The sun's energy may be one of the solutions to our climate change problems. In fact, the sun is responsible for most of the **renewable energy** on Earth. In one day, Earth receives more energy from the sun than the world uses in one year! Let's take a closer look at this amazing star.

Deep in the OCEAN where the SUN never shines lives a type of ORGANISM that can make its own food without sunlight. These organisms use a process called chemosynthesis, which converts chemicals and heat into sugar. The organisms get heat from vents in the floor of the ocean.

SOURCE OF LIFE: THE SUN

WHAT IS A SUN?

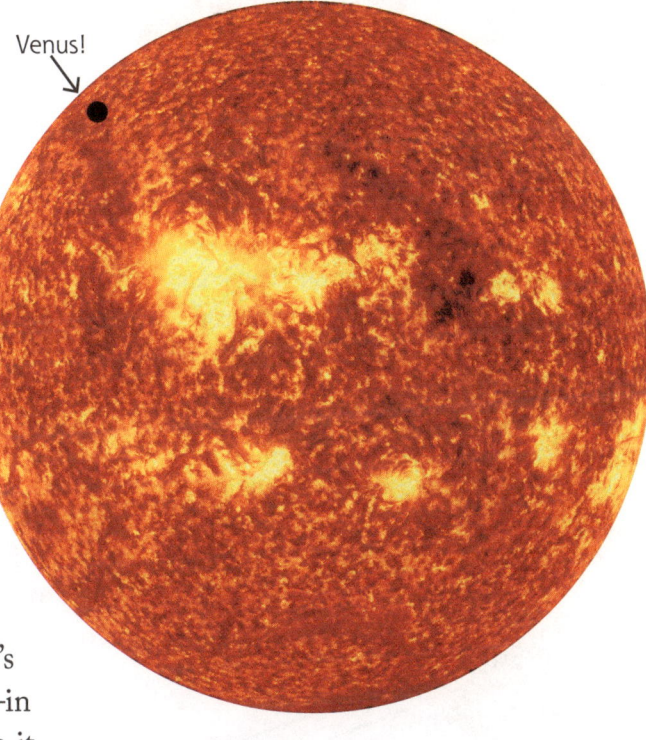

Hello, sun! That's the movement of Venus across the face of the sun.
Credit: NASA Goddard

Our sun is a star that is 4.6 billion years old. It shares similarities with all the other stars in the night sky, except the sun is at the center of our solar system and the other stars are much farther away. This is why the sun looks so big when all the other stars look so small.

The sun contains 99 percent of all the **mass** in the entire solar system! It's the largest object in the solar system—in fact, 1.3 million Earths could fit inside it.

The sun is made of very hot gases—mostly **hydrogen** gas (91 percent) and **helium** gas (8 percent). At the sun's core, hydrogen is **compressed**, which makes it very hot. The temperature in the sun's core is more than 10 million degrees Fahrenheit (5.5 million degrees Celsius). That is more than 12,000 times hotter than Venus! These high temperatures cause the hydrogen atoms to combine and form helium in a reaction known as **nuclear fusion**. Fusion is the source of the sun's energy.

The Color of the Sun

Draw a picture of the sun. What color do you use? Although the sun appears to be yellow to the human eye, it's actually white. White is a mixture of all the colors of the rainbow. When light from the sun goes through our atmosphere, those colors are separated and scattered. Blue and violet light spreads out to make the color of the sky, while the yellows, oranges, and reds stick around to make the sun look yellow.

CLIMATE CHANGE

WORDS TO KNOW

electromagnetic wave: a wave that can travel through the emptiness of space.

speed of light: the speed at which light travels, which is 186,000 miles per second.

sunspot: a dark area on the sun's surface that is cooler than the surrounding area.

hemisphere: half of the earth. North of the equator is called the Northern Hemisphere and south of the equator is the Southern Hemisphere.

equator: an imaginary line around the earth, halfway between the North and South Poles.

Now that we know how the energy in the sun was made, let's look at how it travels to Earth, more than 93 million miles away. The sun's energy travels in **electromagnetic waves**. The word *electromagnetic* means the waves are both electric and magnetic. They move continuously by pushing and pulling on electric and magnetic fields.

All electromagnetic waves travel at the **speed of light**, which is 186,000 miles per second. That is the same as traveling around Earth's equator 7.5 times in 1 second. Sunlight takes 8 minutes and 20 seconds to reach Earth at the speed of light.

If the sun were to magically disappear right now, how long would it take you to know it was gone?

Sunspots

As early as 2,000 years ago, humans noticed dark spots on the sun. You can see these **sunspots** through telescopes. The spots are cooler magnetic areas on the sun that appear in 11-year cycles. Sunspots help scientists study trends and patterns in space to better understand the solar system, including temperature changes here on Earth. Scientists on Earth who have compared the history of sunspots to temperature data on Earth have found that sunspots have been present in both cold and warm temperature time periods. This shows that sunspots are not connected to climate change on Earth.

SOURCE OF LIFE: THE SUN

ADD SOME SEASONING

What season is it right now where you are? Is that the same season someone is having on the other side of the world? Probably not. The seasons help us predict weather and daylight hours during certain times of the year. Seasons are different all over the globe, and it's the planet's relationship with the sun that creates them.

Scientists think of the earth as being divided into two halves, or **hemispheres**, at the **equator**. The top half is called the Northern Hemisphere and the bottom half is the Southern Hemisphere.

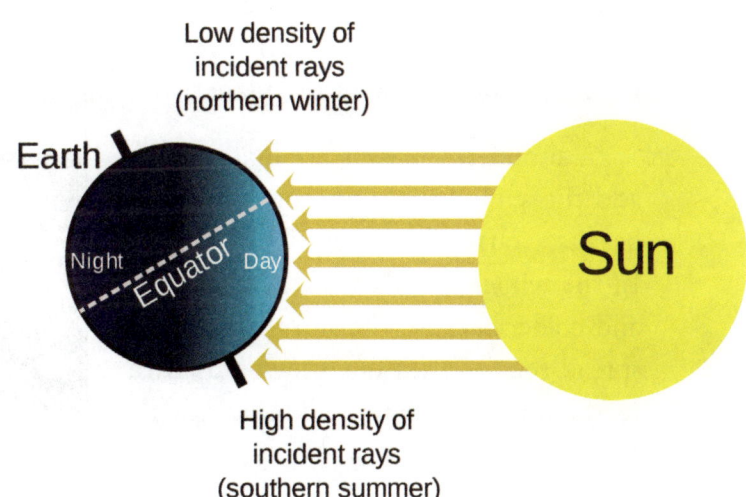

29

CLIMATE CHANGE

WORDS TO KNOW

axis: the imaginary line through the North and South Poles that the earth rotates around.

precipitation: falling moisture in the form of rain, sleet, snow, or hail.

meteorologist: a scientist who studies and forecasts climate and weather.

forecast: a prediction of the weather.

natural disaster: a natural event, such as a fire or flood, that causes great damage.

When it's winter in the Northern Hemisphere, it's summer in the Southern Hemisphere. That means when someone in Boston, Massachusetts, is having fun playing in the snow, someone in Australia is swimming at the beach. The difference in the seasons and the weather patterns of these two hemispheres is because of how the earth travels around the sun.

The earth makes one complete trip around the sun every 365.25 days. This is called Earth's revolution, and it's how we measure a year. Earth's path around the sun, its orbit, is in the shape of an ellipse.

Earth does not rotate around the sun standing straight up. Instead, it's tilted on its **axis** at a 23.5-degree angle. Earth's tilt is the reason for our changing seasons.

The Northern Hemisphere experiences summer when it is tilted toward the sun. The Northern Hemisphere's winter happens when it is tilted away from the sun. This movement around the sun causes a change in the amount and strength of the sunlight that reaches different points on the surface of the planet.

In summer, the days are longer and the sunlight is more concentrated because you're tilted toward the sun. In the winter, the days are shorter and colder because the sun's rays are spread out. The seasons provide us with predictable information about weather.

Having a Looooong Day?

Are days and nights always the same length? How many hours of daylight do you have in a day during the winter? During the summer? That number will depend on where you live. The closer you are to the equator, the less change there is in the amount of daylight.

Enter your own location on this website to see a graph of changing hours of daylight for your area.

🔍 sunrise sunset daylight graph

30

SOURCE OF LIFE: THE SUN

Brrr . . .

Can you guess the coldest temperature recorded on Earth? If you guessed -148 degrees Fahrenheit (-100 degrees Celsius), you are right! This extreme cold is found in Antarctica on an ice ridge between the summits of Dome Argus and Dome Fuji. Compare that to the hottest place on Earth—Death Valley, California, where a temperature of 134 degrees Fahrenheit (56.7 degrees Celsius) has been recorded. What is the temperature difference between these two locations? Is it strange that such extremes can exist on the same planet? It's a big place!

WEATHER OR NOT?

Not only does Earth's relationship to the sun create our seasons, but the sun also impacts weather and climate. Weather is the word we use to describe the conditions that occur during a few hours or days. We usually describe it based on amounts of sunlight, **precipitation**, and temperature. You might look out the window one morning and see that it is rainy and warm. You are noticing the weather. In the fall, you might feel the cold, brisk wind and shorter days of sunlight compared to hot and humid days of summer. We use the weather of the seasons to dress ourselves and plan our outdoor adventures.

Meteorologists study the conditions in our ATMOSPHERE to predict, or forecast, the WEATHER. You have probably seen a meteorologist on television or the internet! Without meteorologists, it would be harder to plan vacations, sporting events, or birthday parties, or prepare for natural disasters.

Climate is a different story. Climate is the average weather during a much longer period of time—decades instead of days. If you live in Arizona, your climate is dry and hot. The weather might include thunderstorms or rain. When scientists study the trends and patterns in climate change, they are looking across many years. These patterns can be found in temperature data or frequency of natural events, such as thunderstorms and wildfires.

31

CLIMATE CHANGE

WORDS TO KNOW

hurricane: a severe tropical storm with winds greater than 74 miles per hour.

drought: a long period of time without rain in places that usually get rain.

solar panel: a device used to capture sunlight and convert it to usable energy.

Climate change affects different places in different ways. For example, the temperatures in the Arctic are rising faster than anywhere on Earth. The temperatures in Antarctica are not changing as fast. Mountain areas are affected differently from coastal areas. Deserts are impacted differently from rainforests.

One symptom of climate change is the increased number of extreme weather events, such as intense **hurricanes**, extended **droughts**, and wildfires. Extreme weather events are natural disasters that cause billions of dollars of economic loss. They are happening all around the world due to climate change, though some regions are being hit harder than others. The National Climate Assessment notes that in the past few years, there has been an increase in multi-months of extreme heat since 1895.

Heavy rainfall events have been occurring at significantly above-average rates since 1991. Even winter is affected by climate change. Winter snow and ice storms have increased in frequency and intensity since the 1950s. The path the storms take is also shifting.

Wildfires are another symptom of climate change. California has seen an uptick in the number and intensity of fires as the region has been plagued by drought. Entire neighborhoods have been wiped out in just a few minutes.

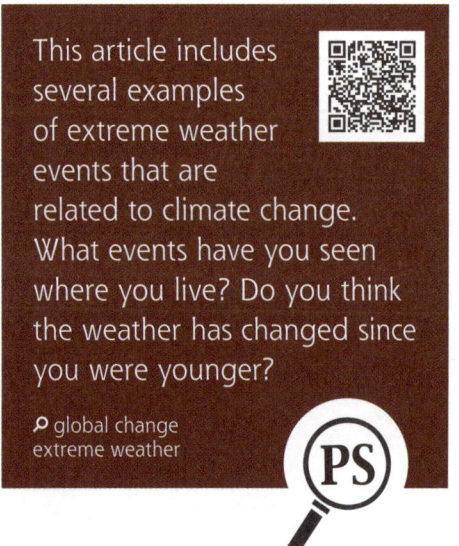

This article includes several examples of extreme weather events that are related to climate change. What events have you seen where you live? Do you think the weather has changed since you were younger?

🔍 global change extreme weather

ENERGY FROM THE SUN

We learned in the introduction that burning fossil fuels for energy releases lots of CO_2 into the atmosphere, which contributes to climate change. Renewable energy technologies are less harmful to our environment.

SOURCE OF LIFE: THE SUN

The energy of the sun is far cleaner, plus it's renewable—it will never run out. Renewable energy from the sun is all around us. Do you see light? You see energy! But . . . how do we harness that energy so we can use it? With **solar panels**.

The first home with solar panels in the United States was built in 1948 in Massachusetts by two women. Physicist Dr. Mária Telkes (1900–1995) and architect Eleanor Raymond (1887–1989) teamed up to build a house with a solar panel roof. This house proved that even in cold climates such as that in Massachusetts, the sun's energy can power a house. Dr. Telkes was known as the "Sun Queen" in the early twentieth century for all of her solar-powered inventions, including solar ovens and water-cleaning systems powered by the sun.

The first SOLAR PANELS on the White House were installed under President Jimmy Carter in 1979.

CLIMATE CHANGE

WORDS TO KNOW

solar array: an arrangement of photovoltaic devices used to collect solar energy to use as electricity.

photoelectric effect: the creation of an electric current after exposure to light.

solar power: energy from the sun converted to electricity.

dense: tightly packed.

atmospheric pressure: the force created by the weight of the atmosphere.

convection current: the movement of hot air rising and cold air sinking.

wind turbine: an engine fitted with blades that are spun around by the wind to generate electricity.

evaporate: to convert from a liquid to a gas.

water cycle: the continuous movement of water from the earth to the clouds and back to the earth again.

Today, solar panels are used widely around the globe. And even in space—the International Space Station has four basketball court-sized **solar arrays**! Solar panels can be found floating in the ocean, standing in deserts, and as bike paths. Scientists and engineers collaborate to bring solar technology to new places.

You might see solar panels as you drive to school—or maybe you even live someplace that has solar panels collecting energy for you to use. Engineers are working to improve the ways we store the sun's energy for use even on cloudy days or during the night.

The sun isn't our only source of renewable energy, but without it, we wouldn't have several other types of energy. Let's see why.

SOURCE OF LIFE: THE SUN

Albert Einstein

Albert Einstein (1879–1955) is one of the greatest scientists of all time. His 1905 discovery of the **photoelectric effect** was important for the development of solar panels. Without his discovery, we would not be able to produce **solar power**. In 1921, Einstein received a Nobel Prize in physics for this work.

WIND, WATER, AND PLANTS

Have you ever been at the beach on a hot day and felt a cool breeze come off the ocean? You can thank the sun! The sun heats the land more quickly than the ocean. The air over land, therefore, is heated more than the air over the water. Warm air rises and cold air sinks, because warm air is less **dense** and lighter than cold air. The rising warm air leaves what's called low **atmospheric pressure**. The cooler air from over the ocean, where there's high atmospheric pressure, rushes in to try to balance the pressure. We feel this **convection current** as wind!

If you've ever seen a **wind turbine**, you've seen the wind's energy captured to generate electricity. The wind is doing the work of spinning the turbines, but the sun was what caused the wind in the first place!

> Check out this video to learn more about how wind turbines harness the energy from a breeze.
>
> 🔍 how do turbines work

The sun is also responsible for the power generated from water. Dams and other technologies convert the energy of water into electricity. Where does this water come from? Energy from the sun warms the water, causing it to **evaporate**, turn into clouds, and come back to the earth as precipitation. This is the **water cycle**. Without the sun, rain and snow would not fall and rivers would not flow.

CLIMATE CHANGE

WORDS TO KNOW

biofuel: fuel made from living matter, such as plants.

algae: a plant-like organism that lives in water and grows by converting energy from the sun into food.

geothermal energy: renewable heat energy that comes from the earth.

nuclear energy: energy made from the splitting of an atom.

fission: the splitting of an atom.

radioactive waste: the dangerous byproduct of nuclear energy.

Biofuels are another alternative energy source. Switchgrass, sugar cane, sugar beets, **algae**, and more can be pressed into a liquid fuel. These biofuels can run our cars, trucks, planes, and boats. The U.S. military is the largest user of biofuel in the world.

The sun provides the energy for these plants to grow and the food that animals eat. We can capture its energy to create heat and electricity for our homes and fuels for our cars. From the tiniest organisms to the largest animals, almost all life relies on the sun for survival.

Only three clean energy solutions are not powered by the sun. **Geothermal energy** comes from heat deep in the earth, tidal energy comes from the tides in the oceans, and **nuclear energy** comes from the splitting of the uranium atom. Nuclear power plants are where nuclear energy is converted into electricity. The splitting of the atom, called **fission**, produces heat, which is used to make steam, which turns a turbine to generate electricity.

From the tiniest ORGANISMS to the largest animals, almost ALL LIFE relies on the sun for survival.

Nuclear power does not add greenhouse gases to our atmosphere, but it does produce a dangerous byproduct called **radioactive waste** that can be very harmful to all life and the environment. This waste has to be cleaned up and concealed, often buried, to keep the planet healthy. Plus, mining for uranium uses a lot of resources.

Every kind of energy source has benefits and disadvantages. Companies and communities need to assess the good and the bad to make the best decisions. In the next chapter, we explore the relationship between the gases in our atmosphere and their effect on the climate.

ESSENTIAL QUESTION

How does the sun affect Earth? Could we have life without the sun?

BUILD YOUR OWN
SUNDIAL

CLIMATE KIT
- paper plate
- half a plastic straw
- drawing materials
- pushpins
- science journal and pencil

How do you tell time? The oldest clock was a sundial. A sundial is also a scientific instrument. Created by Egyptians and used throughout history and even today in many parts of the world, sundials come in all shapes, sizes, and materials. Build your own sundial and mark the change in the sun's shadow to create a timepiece. For best results, do this project on a sunny day.

▶ **Punch a hole in the center of a paper plate.** Don't make the hole bigger than the straw. You want the straw to fit snugly into the hole so it stands up straight.

▶ **Draw the number "12" on any edge of your plate.** Draw a line from the number to the center hole. Use a ruler to keep the line straight!

An ancient sundial

▶ **At noon, stick your half straw into the hole** in the plate and put the plate on the ground. Slowly turn the plate until the shadow of the straw falls on the line to number 12. Secure the sundial to the ground with some pushpins.

▶ **Where do you think the shadow** of the straw will be at 1 p.m., 2 p.m., 3 p.m., and beyond? Draw a small X on the plate where you think the tip of the shadow will be.

▶ **Check the position of the shadow** every hour and trace the outline of the shadow directly onto the plate. Write the number of the hour (1, 2, 3 . . .) on the plate at the end of the shadow. Continue doing this every hour until the sun sets.

▶ **If you want, begin again in the same spot at sunrise** and record the hours until noon to make a complete clock.

▶ **Write down your observations in your science journal.** Why does the shadow seem to be moving? What is actually moving?

Try This!

Research sundials online to see how other people have designed them. Can you find the largest one? How about the smallest? Oldest? How have sundials changed since ancient times?

MAKE AN
APPLE BATTERY

CLIMATE KIT
- handyman multimeter
- AA (1.5-volt) or 9-volt battery
- apple
- copper nail
- zinc-plated nail
- 2 alligator clips
- insulated wire with ends stripped

How do we keep solar energy working at night? Batteries! We use batteries as a way of storing energy. Batteries create electricity from a chemical reaction. A piece of fruit, such as an apple, is an example of nature's battery. The sun's energy is stored in the fruit's sugars and **starches**. We can use those sugars and starches to create electricity.

This project requires a handyman multimeter. This is a scientific instrument that measures **volts**. A volt is the unit used to measure the potential energy, sometimes called stored energy, between two spots in a circuit. The path of a circuit lets electricity flow when it is closed in a loop.

▶ **Start a scientific method worksheet** in your science journal to organize, gather, and analyze your data.

▶ **Practice using your multimeter** with a working AA (1.5-volt) or 9-volt battery to ensure your circuit is properly wired.

▶ **Insert the copper and zinc nails** into the apple, making sure they don't touch or go all the way through the fruit.

Where Do Used Batteries Go?

Many of today's batteries are made out of common metals that are non-hazardous, but that does not mean you should throw them in the trash! Batteries can be recycled. Depending on the metals they're made of, they can be crushed and used in plastic or paper products and even fertilizers. Another option to be even more environmentally friendly is to use rechargeable batteries. These are more expensive to purchase new, but you can recharge them and use them over and over, keeping them out of the recycling centers and landfills and saving money on replacement costs.

❯ **Measure the distance between the nails** and record it in your science journal.

❯ **Connect the wire to both nails with alligator clips** and check the multimeter. How many volts is your apple battery producing? Record your results.

❯ **What do you think will happen** if you put the nails closer together or farther apart? Write your hypothesis in your journal and then place your nails at different distances and record the results. Does the electricity get stronger or weaker? Why?

Try This!

What will happen if the copper and zinc nails are inserted into the apple less or more deeply? What would happen if you change the size of the nails? Record your hypotheses and perform each test. Don't forget to record your results! You can also try using a lemon or potato for a battery. Do you think other fruits or vegetables will be better or worse than the apple?

WORDS TO KNOW

starch: a type of nutrient found in certain foods, such as bread, potatoes, and rice.

volt: the unit used to measure the electric potential between two spots in a circuit.

HOW POWERFUL IS SUNLIGHT?

> **CLIMATE KIT**
> ° dark-colored construction paper
> ° various small toys or objects

We know sunlight helps plants grow, evaporates water, and can burn our skin. We can even generate renewable energy from the sun using solar panels, wind turbines, and other technologies. What else can sunlight do? You need a sunny day to do this activity!

▶ **Put two pieces of paper directly in the sun at or around noon.** Keep a third piece of paper inside.

▶ **Place some toys on one of the pieces of paper** in the sun and trace them with a pencil.

▶ **Organize your predictions in your science journal** using a chart such as the one below. What do you think will happen to the paper? To the objects? Think about the heat and the light from the sun.

	Prediction	Observation After 45 Minutes
Paper in the sun		
Paper in the sun with toys		
Paper out of the sun		

▶ **After 45 minutes, compare the three pieces of construction paper.** How are they different? How are they similar? What caused the differences? On a cloudy day, would it take longer to see any changes?

Try This!

Draw two pictures on two pieces of construction paper using ice cubes. Set one picture in the sun and the other inside for 30 minutes. What happens to the pictures? Why?

BUILD YOUR OWN ANEMOMETER

> **CLIMATE KIT**
> ° 5 paper cups
> ° paint
> ° thin wooden dowels or chopsticks
> ° empty water bottle

Windmills convert the energy in wind to do other types of work. People were harnessing wind power in Greece back in the first century! Here, you are going to make an anemometer, which is a device that measures wind speed.

▶ **Take four paper cups and punch a single hole** halfway down the side of each cup. Paint one cup a color different from the others.

▶ **On the fifth cup, make four holes evenly spaced around the rim.** The first and third holes should be slightly closer to the rim than the second and fourth holes. Carefully punch one hole in the center of the bottom of this cup.

▶ **Slide two of the dowels through the holes** in the fifth cup to make an X. Make sure the first four cups are all on their sides facing the same direction. Connect each through the hole in its side to an end of each of the dowels. Secure each cup to its dowel with tape. Why should they all be facing the same direction?

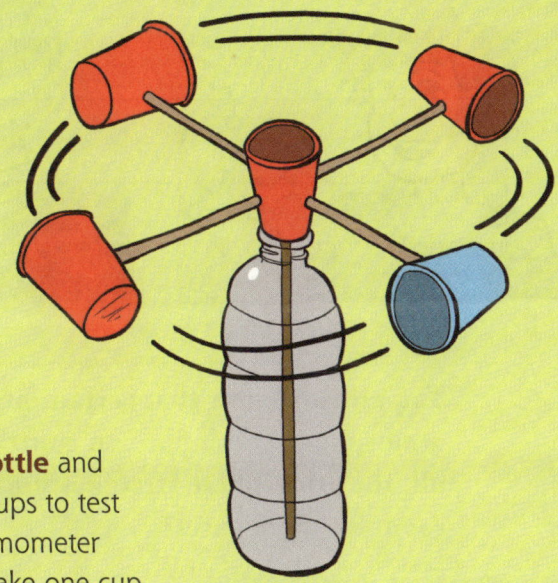

▶ **Insert a dowel through the hole in the bottom** of the fifth cup until it meets the X. Tape the X and the center dowel together.

▶ **Place the center dowel in an empty water bottle** and let the center cup rest on top. Blow into one of the cups to test if your anemometer is working. Then, take your anemometer outside to see if it works in the wind. Why did we make one cup different from the others?

▶ **Record how many rotations your anemometer makes in 30 seconds.** What changes can you make to the windmill to make it spin faster? Record your ideas in your science journal.

Try This!

Design a different anemometer. Does it work better than the original anemometer? Why? How do you know if it works better?

41

Chapter 3

THE POWER OF
GREENHOUSE GASES

You already know that certain human activities release gases into the atmosphere, which in turn contribute to climate change. But why? After all, the atmosphere stretches for miles above Earth—isn't there plenty of room for more gases?

ESSENTIAL QUESTION

Why are the carbon cycle and water cycle important to Earth's climate? What happens when they get disrupted?

One thing that's incredibly important in the atmosphere (and on a spaceship and in your own body) is balance. You've probably tried to balance on a balance beam or fallen log. Sometimes, it takes a lot of effort to stay upright and even! The same is true of our atmosphere. Greenhouse gases need to be balanced. And, sometimes, that takes a lot of effort.

THE POWER OF GREENHOUSE GASES

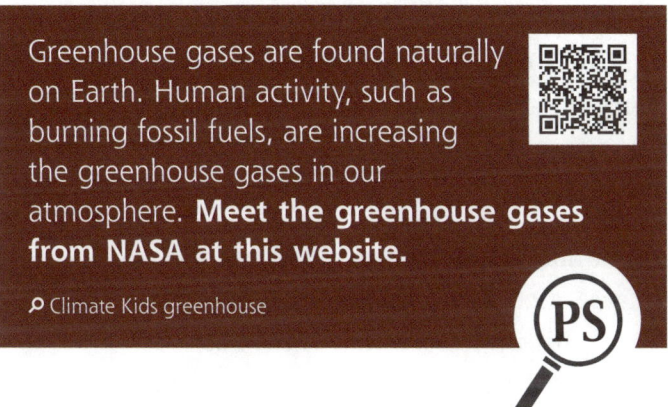

Greenhouse gases are found naturally on Earth. Human activity, such as burning fossil fuels, are increasing the greenhouse gases in our atmosphere. **Meet the greenhouse gases from NASA at this website.**

🔍 Climate Kids greenhouse

> **WORDS TO KNOW**
>
> **enzyme:** a substance in an organism that speeds up the rate of chemical reactions.
>
> **acid:** a sour substance that dissolves some minerals.
>
> **bacteria:** single-celled organisms found in soil, water, plants, and animals. They help decay food and some bacteria are harmful. Singular is bacterium.
>
> **nutrients:** substances in food and soil that living things need to live and grow.

The same is true in your body. Do you ever fart or burp after eating certain foods? During digestion, our bodies produce a special mix of **enzymes** and **acids** called digestive juices that live in our intestines along with billions of **bacteria**. Together, the digestive juices and bacteria break down food so **nutrients** can be carried by our blood and used by our cells.

While creating the energy our bodies need to walk, talk, and grow, this process releases gases. It's normal! However, your digestive system can get out of balance after you eat too much of one kind of food.

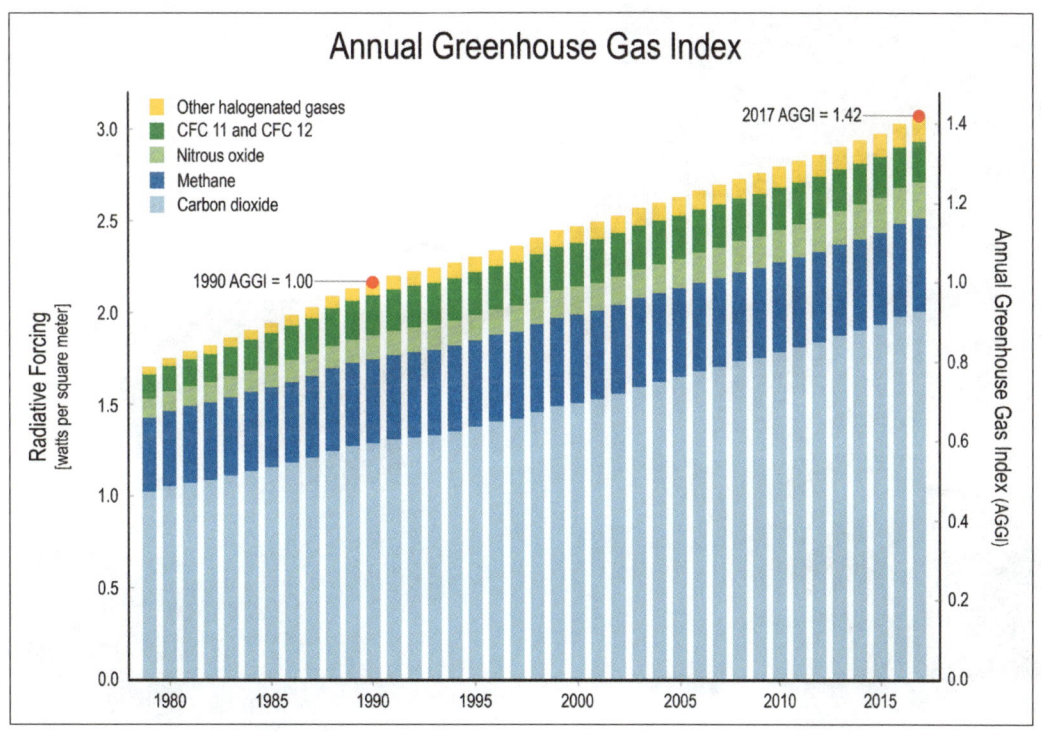

The annual Greenhouse Gas Index shows that levels of greenhouse gases in the atmosphere are increasing.

CLIMATE CHANGE

WORDS TO KNOW

equilibrium: balance.

carbon: an element found in living things, including plants. Carbon is also found in diamonds, charcoal, and graphite.

emission: something sent or given off, such as smoke, gas, heat, or light.

After eating too much birthday cake or soda, you might find that those gases increase and you're burping and farting more than usual. The same thing can happen to the systems on Spaceship Earth.

Many human activities, such as burning fossil fuels, release more greenhouse gases into the atmosphere. It's important that these gases are kept in a careful **equilibrium** because excess greenhouse gases unbalance the climate on Earth. While we need some greenhouse gases in the atmosphere to keep our planet the right temperature to support life, when there are too many, they cause climate change.

The three key greenhouse gases in our atmosphere are methane, water vapor, and CO_2.

The **SUN** is Earth's largest source of **ENERGY**. Yet humans get 90 percent of all energy from burning **FOSSIL FUELS**.

A major source of methane comes from the Arctic region when Arctic ice cracks and breaks and allows methane to escape from the ocean water there.

THE POWER OF GREENHOUSE GASES

METHANE IN THE MIX

Our atmosphere is a mixture of many gases. **Carbon** is present in the atmosphere as CO_2. Methane is another carbon-based gas in our atmosphere. For every molecule of methane in Earth's atmosphere, there are 235 molecules of CO_2. While methane is far less abundant than CO_2, it is a more powerful heat-trapping gas than CO_2. It absorbs 34 times more solar energy than CO_2. Human activities produce less methane than CO_2, but it is important to know how this heat-trapping gas contributes to global warming.

Methane comes from a few different sources. One of the largest sources gives us steak and hamburgers. More than 1.5 billion cows live on our planet—these creatures release massive amounts of methane as they digest their food. Cows burp and fart just like humans, and they release methane when they burp and fart. In fact, they are one of the world's largest producers of methane. Combine their gases with that from other livestock animals, such as sheep, pigs, and chickens, and that's a lot of methane going into the air. Scientists are exploring ways to reduce and capture this methane.

From feeding cows garlic and curry to capturing METHANE GAS with methane digesters, we can reduce the amount of methane that is released into the ATMOSPHERE.

The burning of fossil fuels is another way methane gets released into the atmosphere. Natural gas and oil systems are the largest sources of methane **emissions** in the United States. We use natural gas to heat our homes and fuel our stoves. We use oil for transportation and the generation of electricity. Methane is released into the atmosphere during the production, transportation, storage, and use of both these systems.

CLIMATE CHANGE

WORDS TO KNOW

decompose: to rot or decay.

respiratory system: the parts of the body used to breathe.

regulate: to control or to keep steady.

photosynthesis: the process by which plants produce food, using light as energy.

evolve: to change or develop gradually.

One stinky source of methane is our trash as it **decomposes** in landfills. Landfills are the third-largest source of methane emissions in the United States. As more and more people throw out more stuff, what do you think will happen to methane levels in our atmosphere?

Remember, small changes in the amount of greenhouse gases can upset the balance in the atmosphere. It's the same way small changes in your diet can affect how you feel.

METHANE DIGESTERS are being used to convert cow manure into **ELECTRICITY** and **FERTILIZER**. Manure is heated up and turned into liquid, which releases the **METHANE GAS**. This gas is captured and burned to produce electricity. The remaining manure is separated to be turned into fertilizer.

THE POWER OF GREENHOUSE GASES

CARBON DIOXIDE IN THE AIR

Take a deep breath and blow it back out. What's happening? Where is the air going? What parts of our body are doing the work? We breathe all day, every day, without thinking much about it. Your **respiratory system** keeps you alive by breathing in oxygen to create energy and breathing out CO_2 as a waste product. All animals have respiratory systems that breathe in oxygen and release CO_2.

Planet Earth has a respiratory system, too. The forests and oceans act as lungs to help **regulate** the balance of gases in our atmosphere. But there's a big difference. Plants absorb CO_2 to make energy in a process known as **photosynthesis**. They release their waste product, oxygen, during a process known as respiration. Life on Earth has **evolved** to produce two perfectly interconnected systems! Plants produce what humans and animals need, and humans and animals breathe out what plants need.

Go outside and look at the biggest tree you can find. Trees grow just as you do, with energy they gain from nutrients in the soil, water, and sunlight. Trees grow taller and wider by absorbing CO_2 from the air during photosynthesis.

CLIMATE CHANGE

WORDS TO KNOW

boreal forest: a northern forest filled mostly with conifers, which are trees with needles that produce cones.

agriculture: growing crops and raising animals for food.

habitat: the natural area where a plant or animal lives.

carbon cycle: the way carbon is exchanged between the atmosphere and Earth's ecosystems.

Every tree ring shows carbon being stored.

That big tree outside your window contains thousands of pounds of carbon that it has absorbed right out of the air. A healthy tree can absorb up to 50 pounds of CO_2 from the atmosphere every year. Just like methane, CO_2 needs to be balanced in the atmosphere. Too much carbon in one place, such as in the ocean or in the air, has consequences for the entire earth. Planting trees and preserving forests can help us remove excess CO_2 from our atmosphere.

> When a tree **BURNS,** all its trapped **CARBON** is released back into the **ATMOSPHERE.**

Scientists and citizens alike are very concerned about protecting current forests, such as the Amazon rainforest in South America, the Cloud Forest in Costa Rica, and Canada's **boreal forests**. Yet, sadly, we are destroying millions of acres of forestland each year, cutting down trees for paper and fuel and clearing the forests for **agriculture**. Giant wildfires further damage these delicate ecosystems. This means our planet's lungs are getting smaller while at the same time we are releasing more and more CO_2 into the atmosphere.

Tree cover around the world

Credit: NASA Earth Observatory/Image by Jesse Allen and Robert Simmon/Based on data from Michael Lefsky

THE POWER OF GREENHOUSE GASES

Joseph Black and Joseph Priestley

In 1754, Joseph Black (1728–1799) discovered the existence of CO_2. Twenty years later, another scientist, named Joseph Priestley (1733–1804), discovered oxygen. Without these two discoveries, we'd still believe that air is one single substance. Black also discovered that CO_2 is denser than air and can put out fire. Today, we use CO_2 in fire extinguishers.

One way an individual citizen can take positive action to help the climate is to plant a tree. One tree produces enough oxygen for four people to breathe. During a tree's life, it can absorb thousands of pounds of CO_2 from the air. Trees provide us with shade and **habitats** for animals and birds. They also absorb excess water.

The process of adding and subtracting CARBON from Earth's atmosphere is part of the carbon cycle.

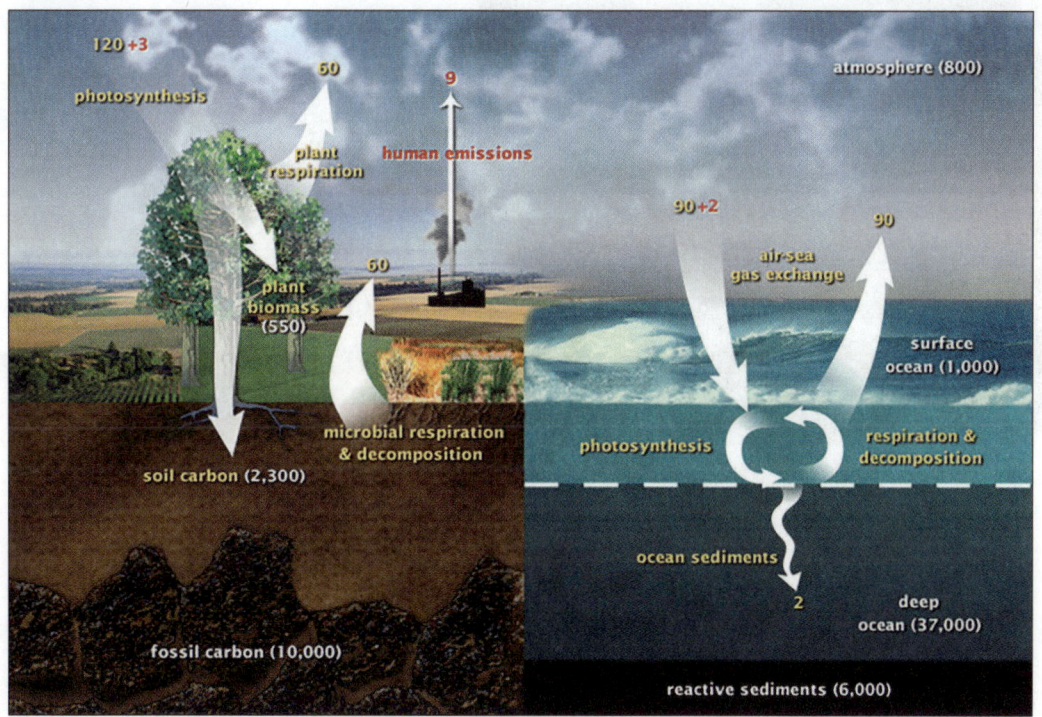

The carbon cycle

Credit: adapted from U.S. DOE, Biological and Environmental Research Information System

CLIMATE CHANGE

WORDS TO KNOW

calcium: a mineral found in shells and bones.

phytoplankton: microscopic, drifting plants, such as algae, that live in both fresh water and salt water.

sedimentary rock: rock formed from the compression of sediments, the remains of plants and animals, or the evaporation of seawater.

limestone: a kind of rock that forms from the skeletons and shells of sea creatures. Limestone can also form through precipitation of calcium and carbonate.

CARBON DIOXIDE IN THE WATER

Oceans are another part of Earth's respiratory system. They play an extremely important role in absorbing CO_2 from our atmosphere.

Anywhere that air touches the surface of water, a few molecules of CO_2 dissolve in the water. Since water covers 70 percent of Earth's surface, that leads to 1.7 gigatons of carbon dioxide being absorbed annually. That's the same as the weight of 85,000,000 blue whales!

What happens to the CO_2 absorbed by the ocean? Many ocean organisms use it to help them make **calcium** carbonate to create their shells. Have you ever walked down the beach and collected shells? Those are formed from carbon!

CO_2 is also absorbed by tiny organisms called **phytoplankton**. Phytoplankton are marine algae that can be found in many parts of the ocean. Often they are found floating on the surface of the water. As all plants do, they absorb carbon dioxide and release oxygen. Phytoplankton are so abundant in the ocean that they can be seen from space! They are responsible for producing 50 percent of the oxygen we breathe.

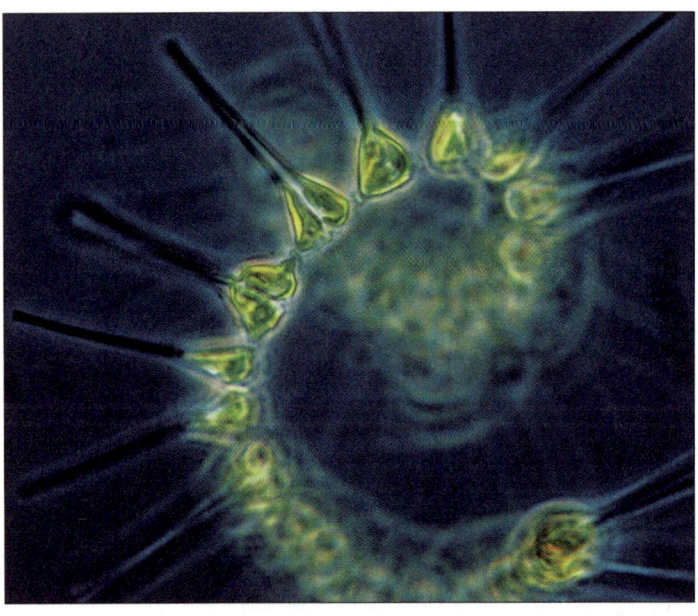

Phytoplankton are the foundation of the ocean's food web.
Credit NOAA MESA Project

THE POWER OF GREENHOUSE GASES

Most CO_2 that is not used by life forms in the ocean sinks slowly to the bottom, where it accumulates in layers of **sedimentary rock**. After millions of years, this large accumulation of carbon on the ocean floor turns into rock known as **limestone**. Limestone is found all over the planet.

THE WATER CYCLE

Some of the most famous **LIMESTONE** cliffs in the world are the White Cliffs of Dover in Dover, England. These cliffs are evidence of the massive amounts of **CARBON** that our **OCEANS ABSORB**.

The water cycle plays an important role in regulating Earth's temperature. Water is in continuous movement above and below the surface of Earth. Because of the water cycle, the water you drink today could be the same water the dinosaurs swam in and drank more than 65 million years ago.

Energy from the sun transports water from one place to another and changes its state between liquid, solid, and gas, depending on the amount of heat in the water. Oceans, lakes, and drinking cups contain liquid water. Ice trays and glaciers contain solid water. The atmosphere contains water vapor, which makes clouds, rain, and snow.

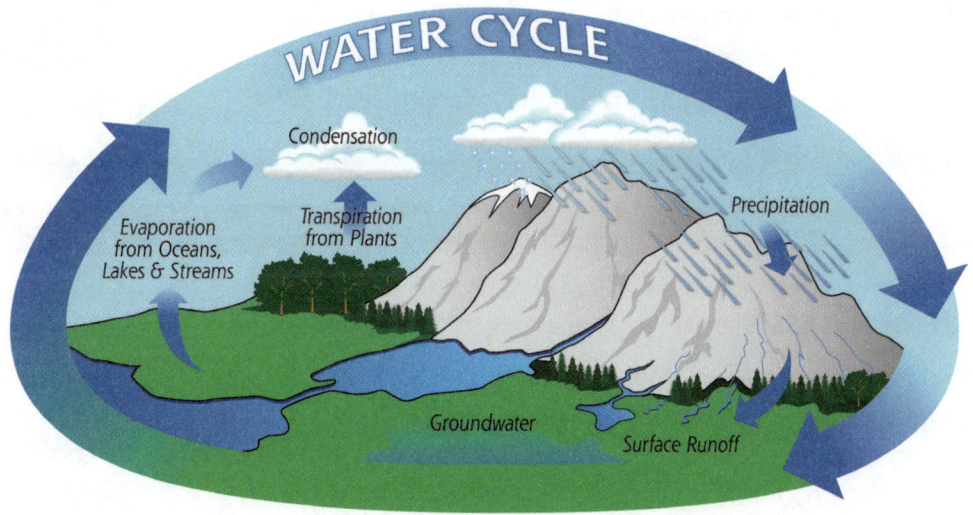

The water cycle
Credit: NASA

CLIMATE CHANGE

WORDS TO KNOW

condense: to change from a gas to a liquid.

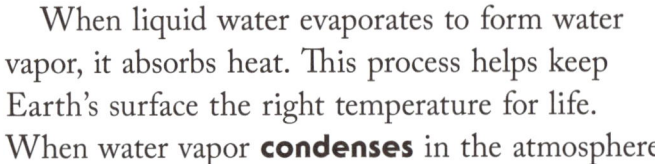

When liquid water evaporates to form water vapor, it absorbs heat. This process helps keep Earth's surface the right temperature for life. When water vapor **condenses** in the atmosphere to form precipitation, it releases heat. The releasing of this heat also helps to regulate temperature. Water vapor in Earth's atmosphere absorbs and reflects much of the sun's energy. That is why water vapor is also considered a greenhouse gas. Remember, we need greenhouse gases for life on Earth, but we need them in the right amounts.

It might sound strange that water helps to both heat and cool Earth, but as long as the system stays balanced, Earth stays the right temperature. Small changes in our climate can have significant impacts on the water cycle. This means that some places might be affected by drought. Coastal areas could see rising sea levels, which could eventually drive large numbers of people inland. These changes in the water cycle also increase the risk of more torrential rains and inland flooding. Such consequences would affect our ability to produce food and energy.

What happens when systems get out of balance? In the next chapter, we will explore changes in our climate. By understanding our ancient climates, we can see how human activities are disrupting our atmosphere's balance.

ESSENTIAL QUESTION

Why are the carbon cycle and water cycle important to Earth's climate? What happens when they get disrupted?

Sweat It Out!

Do you get sweaty when you exercise? That's your body's way of regulating its temperature. When the sweat on your skin evaporates, it absorbs heat, just like water absorbs heat when it evaporates into the atmosphere. Your body cools off, just like Earth cools off, through evaporation.

EXPERIMENT WITH
DRY ICE

CLIMATE KIT
- tongs
- rubber gloves
- safety goggles
- dry ice
- 2 plates
- 2 glasses
- dish soap
- food coloring

The North and South Poles of Mars have ice caps just as the poles of Earth have ice caps. The ice on Mars, however, is much different. On Earth, polar ice is made of frozen water. On Mars, polar ice is made of frozen CO_2. To learn about CO_2 as both a solid and a gas, experiment with dry ice. Like the polar ice on Mars, dry ice is made from frozen CO_2.

Caution: Have an adult work with you when you experiment with dry ice. Dry ice can cause frostbite if you touch it with your skin. Wear safety goggles and rubber gloves and use tongs to move dry ice.

▶ **You can purchase dry ice at most grocery stores,** although you may have to call in advance. Buy the dry ice the day you plan to use it and carry it in an open bucket, not an airtight container. Open the windows while in the car to keep fresh oxygen in the air. The clouds that form when working with dry ice are safe for you to touch and feel. Do not touch the ice itself.

▶ **Start a scientific method worksheet in your science journal.** What can you learn about CO_2 from experimenting with dry ice? Make your prediction.

▶ **Use tongs and wear gloves to place a piece of dry ice on a plate.** Place a piece of regular ice on a different plate. Leave the ice for one hour. What happens? Why do you think frozen CO_2 is called dry ice? Record your observations.

▶ **Fill a glass halfway with warm water.** Use the tongs and gloves to place a piece of dry ice in the glass. What happens? Add more warm water to the glass after a couple of minutes and observe the results.

▶ **Add a squirt of liquid dish soap to the warm water.** How does this change the behavior of the dry ice?

▶ **Add food coloring to the glass of water.** What happens to the gas? Record your observations in your science journal.

Explore Mars! NASA has images, videos, mosaics, and data from the rovers that are exploring the red planet.

🔍 Mars rover

MEASURE THE
MOISTURE IN THE AIR

CLIMATE KIT
- jar with lid
- freezer

What does your skin feel like on a hot, sticky day? Moist and wet? That's because of moisture in the air. We call this moisture humidity. You can find evidence of moisture in the air with this experiment.

▶ **Start a scientific method worksheet.** What will happen to a jar of air when you heat it up or cool it down? Record your hypothesis. What will this tell you about the moisture in the air?

▶ **Put the lid on your jar and place it in a shady spot outside for about 10 minutes.** Observe what happens to the air inside the jar during this time and record what you notice.

▶ **Freeze your jar for 90 minutes, then set it on a table.** It will be really cold! What do you see? What happened to the air inside the jar? What does this tell you about the amount of moisture?

▶ **Record your observations in your science journal.** Compare your results to your predictions.

Try This!

Repeat this experiment in different locations at different temperatures. Try different types of containers. What happens?

The amount of WATER VAPOR in the air varies, depending on the CLIMATE on the ground. Where do you think you'll find the most water vapor in the air? The least?

DECOMPOSITION EXPERIMENT

CLIMATE KIT
° 3 plastic Ziploc bags
° soil
° banana peel

We have all heard that plastic takes longer to decompose than *organic* materials. Plastic straws, for example, can last 500 years in a landfill. A banana peel will last a few days to a few weeks. When food and waste decompose, they release methane and other greenhouse gases into the atmosphere. In this experiment, we will see how food wrapped in plastic decomposes.

❯ **Put soil in one bag, and bury a piece of banana peel in the center.**

❯ **Put another piece of banana peel into a second Ziploc plastic bag.** Close it tight with no air inside. Then, put the banana in the bag into the third bag and cover it with soil.

❯ **Write down your hypothesis of what you think will happen.** Wait 7 to 10 days. Open both bags and see the difference in the decomposition of the two pieces of banana peel. Record your results.

How Long Is It Around?

You might think that aluminum soda can is simply gone once you've tossed it in the trash, but guess what? That can is going to be around for a long, long time. Take a look at how long these common items take to decompose.

- › Glass bottle, 1 million years
- › Plastic beverage bottles, 450 years
- › Disposable diapers, 450 years
- › Tin cans, 50 years
- › Nylon fabric, 30–40 years
- › Plastic bag, 10–20 years
- › Waxed milk carton, 3 months
- › Apple core, 2 months
- › Newspaper, 6 weeks
- › Orange or banana peel, 2–5 weeks

Try This!

Compare the decomposition rates of different objects by repeating the experiment in soil.

WORDS TO KNOW

organic: something that is or was living, such as animals, wood, grass, and insects. Also refers to food grown naturally, without chemicals.

Chapter 4

EXAMINE AN
ANCIENT CLIMATE

The climate today is very different from the climate the dinosaurs experienced. We know that Earth's climate is constantly changing, but what's the best way to find clues about our planet's past climate? By traveling back in time!

Scientists travel back in time in many ways. They examine **fossils** to see what lived at different times in the past. They study gases trapped in ice to learn about ancient atmospheres. They read the clues written in **coral reefs**, muddy ocean floors, and **tree rings** to understand climate at different points in time.

Why is it important to study the climate of the past? How does understanding the past help us understand the present?

ESSENTIAL QUESTION

How do scientists learn about Earth's climate as it was billions of years ago?

EXAMINE AN ANCIENT CLIMATE

Scientists gather data about ancient environments so they can better understand today's climate. Let's begin by going back in time to when most of Earth was covered in ice.

WORDS TO KNOW

fossil: the remains or traces of an ancient plant or animal left in rock.

coral reef: an underwater ecosystem made by coral. Coral is an organism with a hard, outer calcium carbonate skeleton.

tree ring: a layer of wood added inside a tree each year as it grows.

glacier: a slowly moving mass of ice and snow.

glaciologist: a scientist who studies glaciers.

ICY TIMES

Today, there are **glaciers** on every continent except Australia. The oldest glaciers in the world are in Antarctica and Greenland. In the United States, glaciers can be found in Montana, Wyoming, Colorado, Idaho, Nevada, Washington, Alaska, and even California! Alaska alone has more than 616 named glaciers. The biggest glacier in North America—the Bering Glacier—is found in Alaska.

This might sound like a lot of glaciers, but glaciers once covered much more of Earth than they do today. Now, glaciers are far fewer, and those that remain are smaller. This shrinkage is due to climate change. **Glaciologists** study the remaining glaciers to learn about Earth's changing climate.

CLIMATE CHANGE

WORDS TO KNOW

striation: a pattern of parallel grooves or narrow bands.

ice core: a sample of ice taken out of a glacier, used to study climate.

Industrial Revolution: a period of time beginning in the late 1700s when people started using machines to make things in large factories.

technology: the tools, methods, and systems used to solve a problem or do work.

parts per million (ppm): a common measurement of pollution in the air.

Glaciers may seem very still, but they are always moving. As they move, glaciers deposit rocks and leave scrapes on the surface of the earth. These rock piles and scrapes help scientists understand the direction the glacier traveled and how far it went.

Have you ever been to Central Park in New York City? You can see the glacial scrapes, called **striations**, on rocks there. Long Island, New York, was formed by a giant glacier thousands of years ago. As the glacier melted, it left behind an enormous pile of rocks that is now Long Island. Scientists have mapped glacial movement around the globe to better understand climate change.

The **FROZEN** parts of **EARTH** are called the cryosphere.

One way scientists study ancient climates is by drilling down into glaciers or ice shelves and collecting **ice core** samples. They analyze gas bubbles in the ice cores to measure the amount of greenhouse gases that were present in the atmosphere in the past, as far back as 800,000 years ago.

The Industrial Revolution

The **Industrial Revolution** is the period of time starting in the 1700s and lasting through the early 1900s when factories began to flourish and people moved from an agricultural way of life to an urban way of life. It used to be that people lived in villages and made their own tools and grew their own food or exchanged goods with immediate neighbors. As **technology** advanced and people learned to better harness energy such as coal, factories were able to mass produce the items people used to make themselves, including clothing, furniture, and building supplies. People began to move to cities from the countryside, creating a need for a denser style of housing. All that technological advancement took its toll with increased levels of air and water pollution.

EXAMINE AN ANCIENT CLIMATE

NASA scientists collect ice core samples from the South Pole.
Credit: NASA

The ice core data shows that during the last 800,000 years, until around the 1850s, the amount of CO_2 in the atmosphere remained below 300 **parts per million (ppm)**. Since then, CO_2 levels have jumped nearly 45 percent, from 250 ppm in the 1850s to more than 400 ppm.

The *JOIDES Resolution* studies both mud and ice to learn about past climates. **Look at this video about collecting and studying core samples.**

🔎 JOIDES Resolution Antarctica

Air bubbles trapped in glaciers tell us that more greenhouse gases are in the atmosphere now than at any time during the past 800,000 years. This imbalance of greenhouse gases in the atmosphere is causing climate change, which is melting glaciers around the globe.

CLIMATE CHANGE

> **WORDS TO KNOW**
>
> **elevation:** the height above sea level.
>
> **polyp:** a small creature that lives in colonies and forms coral.
>
> **plankton:** microscopic plants and animals that float or drift in great numbers in bodies of water.
>
> **conservationist:** a person who works to preserve nature.

GLACIERS behave like a **SLOW-MOVING RIVER.** Just like a river, **GRAVITY** is pulling the glacier from a higher **elevation** to a lower elevation, which is why they move. Just a lot slower. The **FASTEST** recorded glacier moved **47 METERS A DAY.**

As the glaciers melt, they add large amounts of water to the oceans, causing the sea level to rise—so far by more than 6 inches. Melting glaciers are a problem for anyone who lives near a coastline, which is more than half of Earth's inhabitants. Some scientists have predicted that up to 70 percent of all glaciers could melt by 2100.

CORAL REEFS

Coral reefs are one of the oldest, most diverse ecosystems on the planet. Coral reefs are made from tiny organisms called corals, which settle on rocks and form hard shells of calcium.

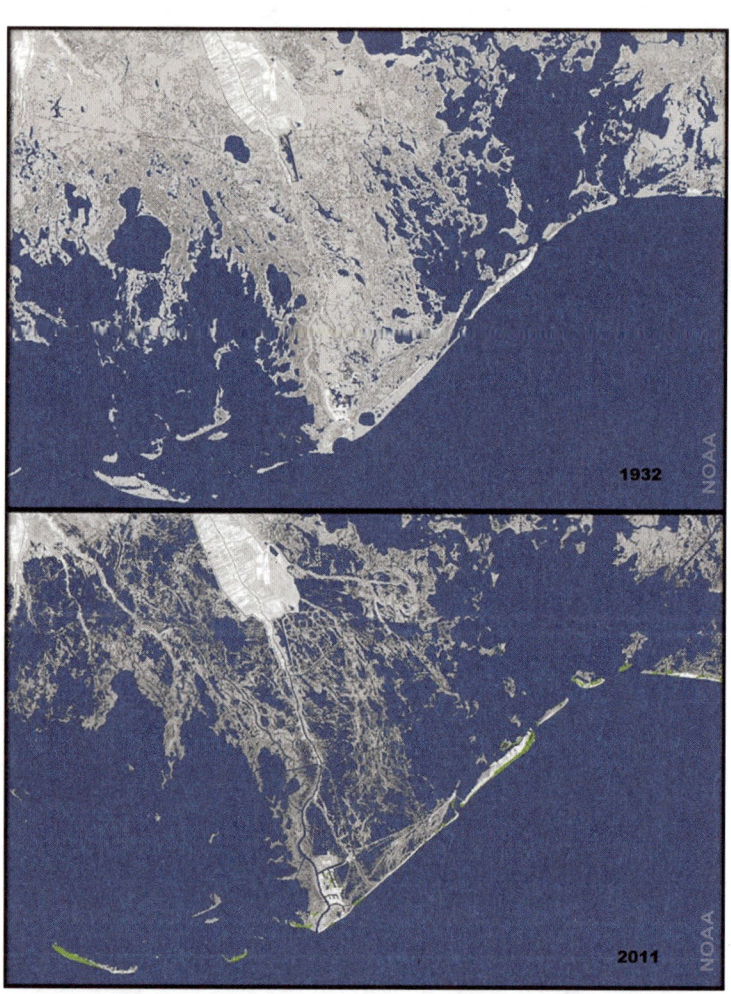

Compare the amount of land on the Louisiana coastline from 1932 to 2011. What might happen if that trend continues?

Credit: NOAA

EXAMINE AN ANCIENT CLIMATE

Richard Alley

Glaciologist Richard Alley (1957–) has drilled 2 miles down into Greenland's glaciers! His team works in below-freezing temperatures to pull up ice cores from 110,000 years ago. Can you imagine a glacier that is 2 miles thick? Picture 34 Statues of Liberty stacked on top of each other. The island country of Greenland is covered in glaciers. What happens if Greenland's glaciers all melt into the sea?

Millions of individual corals, called **polyps**, settle in large groups. As time passes, their small, hard skeletons grow like layers on a tree, making huge structures that are home to colorful algae, **plankton**, and fish.

Called the rainforests of the ocean, coral reefs are found in shallow, warm waters near the equator. Coral reefs are home to nearly 4,000 species of fish and more than 800 species of hard and soft corals. Many of the organisms that live there can't survive if the ocean temperature increases or decreases by even a few degrees.

Corals are among the oldest known living marine organisms. Scientists have found 4,000-year-old coral colonies in Australia. Coral reefs are also found in the Philippines, Hawaii, Palau, the Mariana Islands, Belize, and around the world.

The OCEAN is the largest unexamined place on EARTH—less than 5 PERCENT of it has been EXPLORED.

Scientists and **conservationists** are collaborating to build coral farms. Some coral farms are found on land and some are underwater gardens. Scientists are exploring techniques to help speed up the growth of corals and testing which corals grow best in different conditions. Remember, even the land-based coral farms are still using sunlight and a constant flow of seawater. **You can learn more about growing coral reefs in this video.**

🔍 Atlantic coral reef revival

CLIMATE CHANGE

> **WORDS TO KNOW**
>
> **coral band:** a layer added each year to coral reefs.
>
> **ocean acidification:** the process by which the ocean absorbs CO_2 from the atmosphere, and through a series of chemical reactions, becomes more acidic.
>
> **coral bleaching:** coral that turns white, indicating it is ill and dying.

The extremely long lifespans of coral reefs make them a wonderful place to study changes in climate. Scientists study coral reefs in a variety of ways—through observation, collecting samples, and chemical analysis.

Scientists are using an instrument called the portable remote imaging spectrometer (PRISM) to take pictures and data of coral reefs around the globe. In a photo, the reefs look turquoise, the waves appear to be white, and the brown lines represent the edge of the coral reefs. Scientists can also figure out how deep the water is based on the shades of blue where the corals grow.

When observing corals up close, scientists look for changes in color and size as indicators of health. Corals get their color from algae that live in their tissues. These algae give coral reefs a wide range of beautiful colors. When corals lose that color, scientists know they're unhealthy.

> **Take a tour of PRISM and learn what scientists are doing to study coral reefs.** You can see some photos of what's going on in coral reefs, too.
>
> 🔎 coral prism video

CORAL REEFS are built by one of the slowest-growing **ORGANISMS** on **EARTH,** growing 2 to 3 centimeters a year. That's slower than your fingernails! **THE GREAT BARRIER REEF** is 1,553 miles long and the **RED SEA CORAL REEF** is 1,180 miles long. Scientists estimate that it took these two reefs more than 100,000 years to grow to their current sizes.

EXAMINE AN ANCIENT CLIMATE

Scientists also take samples of living and dead corals. They compare the thickness of **coral bands** to data on CO_2 in the atmosphere. Thinner coral layers indicate slower growth. Remember that oceans absorb massive amounts of carbon dioxide, just as our forests do.

Increases in carbon dioxide in the atmosphere lead to increases in carbon dioxide absorption by the ocean and to **ocean acidification**. Ocean acidification causes coral bands to grow more slowly, making them thinner.

Global warming is also causing changes to ocean temperatures and sea levels. Warming water temperatures and increased acidity harm the algae in coral reefs, causing them to lose color and even die. This is called **coral bleaching** because the coral turns white.

> You can see the largest coral reef from outer space! The Australian Great Barrier Reef stretches more than 1,500 miles.
> Credit: NASA

CLIMATE CHANGE

> **WORDS TO KNOW**
>
> **microfossil:** a tiny fossil that can be seen only with a microscope.
>
> **diatom:** a type of algae found in both water and soil.

Coral bleaching can stunt the growth of coral, leave it exposed to disease, and even kill it. Nearly 60 percent of coral reefs around the world are at risk of coral bleaching.

As of 2017, half of the Great Barrier Reef was already bleached. Additionally, rising sea levels reduce the amount of sunlight reaching corals, which is another factor that impacts their growth. Studying coral growth helps scientists understand how changing conditions in the atmosphere are changing conditions in the ocean.

> You can see coral bleaching for yourself in this video.
>
> 🔍 Nat Geo coral bleaching

Bleached coral
Credit: pvandyke3 (CC BY 2.0)

EXAMINE AN ANCIENT CLIMATE

MUD PIES FROM THE DEEP SEA

On a hot summer's day, it's fun to wade in the ocean and feel squishy, cool mud between your toes. If you pull up a handful of that mud, you might find small rocks and pieces of seashells. The mud also has tiny shells that you can't see. These are called **microfossils**.

Using state-of-the-art equipment, scientists drill into the ocean floor, much like glaciologists drill into glaciers. They collect mud cores to study. Scientists pay extra-close attention to the microfossils at each layer in the cores. Looking at the tiny shells found at different depths tells us about Earth's changing climate.

The chemistry of shells from tiny microscopic animals, such as **diatoms**, gives us clues about ocean temperatures, wind patterns, and sea levels. Diatoms are a type of algae that act as early indicators of the impact of climate change, including changes in sea level. As the temperature of water changes, so does the population of diatoms.

DIATOMS can be found in both deep-water and shallow-water areas.

65

CLIMATE CHANGE

WORDS TO KNOW

dendrochronology: the study of tree rings.

avalanche: a sudden and quick downhill flow of snow and ice from a mountain.

paleontologist: a scientist who studies plant and animal fossils.

fossil record: a record of information of the past that a collection of fossils can provide.

Mesozoic era: a period of time from about 252 to 66 million years ago, when dinosaurs roamed the earth.

geologist: a scientist who studies the history, structure, and origin of the earth.

stromatolite: a type of blue-green algae that uses photosynthesis to make its own food.

cyanobacteria: bacteria that use photosynthesis, better known as blue-green algae.

Since the 1850s, diatom communities have changed dramatically in Arctic waters. Their silica shells have become more delicate and fragile as the oceans have become more acidic. The softer, weaker shells have made it more difficult for diatoms to survive.

How far into the past can we travel with mud? It all depends on the type of water. In fresh water, every 3 feet of mud can be equal to 1,000 years! Next time you walk into a lake, remember you could dig down and touch mud that could be a thousand years old. Saltwater oceans and seas accumulate layers of mud more slowly. In the deep ocean, a half inch of mud equals a thousand years. How long a core sample would equal 10,000 years?

RINGS OF TIME

A sequoia tree named General Sherman grows in California.
Credit: Jim Bahn (CC BY 2.0)

Trees can live to be more than 5,000 years old. In California, a giant Sequoia tree named the President is 3,200 years old! As a tree grows older, each year it adds a new layer of wood, a tree ring. Tree rings show evidence of changes in the environment just as ice and mud do. Scientists study tree rings to estimate temperatures on Earth before climate measurements were recorded. This study of tree rings is called **dendrochronology**.

DENDRON = tree, **chronos** = time, and **logos** = the study of.

EXAMINE AN ANCIENT CLIMATE

Dendrochronologists examine trees and stumps or they drill into a tree and pull out a core, just as glaciologists take core samples from glaciers. First, scientists count the tree rings to determine the tree's age. Then, they measure the thickness of the rings, which provides information about the precipitation and temperature that occurred during that year. For example, a wet season causes thicker tree rings and a dry season causes thinner tree rings. Changes in temperature can also affect the thickness of a tree ring. Tree rings reveal past **avalanches**, landslides, earthquakes, and insect outbreaks.

GIANT SEQUOIAS have recorded the fires that happened during the last 3,000 years.

WALKING WITH DINOSAURS

Paleontologists can reconstruct Earth's climate history from millions and even billions of years ago by looking at the **fossil record**. Through fossils, scientists know that some of the coldest places on Earth were once tropical rainforests! Fossil ferns from the **Mesozoic era** have been found in places that are cold today. These ferns could not have survived freezing temperatures. Scientists believe there were probably no glaciers during the time of the dinosaurs.

With NOAA's Data in the Classroom, students use real-time ocean data to explore today's most pressing environmental issues and develop problem-solving skills employed by scientists. **Check out these classroom-ready curriculum activities with a scaled approach to learning and easy-to-use data exploration tools.**

🔍 NOAA data in the classroom

Geologists can even travel back more than 2 billion years to the era before the first animals lived, when Earth's atmosphere had almost no oxygen. They do this by studying fossils of **stromatolites**, one of the oldest organisms in Earth's history.

Stromatolites are a type of blue-green algae that use photosynthesis to make their own food. They are formed by the growth of layer upon layer of **cyanobacteria**, a type of bacteria that still exists today.

CLIMATE CHANGE

WORDS TO KNOW

paleoclimatology: the study of ancient climates.

Paleoclimatology is the study of ANCIENT CLIMATES using information collected from tree rings, ice cores, coral, and mud.

Geologists have found fossils of stromatolites from 2 billion years ago all around the globe. What happened 2 billion years ago? Almost overnight, the amount of oxygen in our atmosphere increased because stromatolites started releasing oxygen into the air, just as trees do now!

Glaciers, coral reefs, mud, and trees provide lots of information about Earth's climate. They show that although the climate has always gone through changes, today's climate change is happening much, much more quickly than it ever has before.

Since the beginning of the Industrial Revolution, humans have released large amounts of greenhouse gases into the atmosphere from burning fossil fuels. Scientists have found evidence that this is responsible for climate change. In less than 150 years, the concentrations of carbon dioxide in the atmosphere have increased 45 percent. Remember what happens with too much CO_2 in the atmosphere? Our Earth is out of balance.

ESSENTIAL QUESTION

How do scientists learn about Earth's climate as it was billions of years ago?

Credit: fvanrenterghem (CC BY 2.0)

FOSSIL COLLECTION

CLIMATE KIT
- ½ cup flour
- ½ cup used coffee grounds
- ¼ cup salt
- ¼ cup sand
- small objects such as shells, rocks, plastic toys, or leaves
- magnifying glass

Fossils are the remains or impressions of plants or animals that lived long ago, preserved in rock. They provide clues about ancient life. You can create your own fossils of objects you have collected. Make your own fossil dough or purchase plaster of Paris.

❯ **Mix all the dry ingredients together.** Make a thick dough by adding a little water. You want a dough that isn't crumbly or too sticky.

❯ **On a flat surface, knead the dough** and press it into a slab an inch or two thick.

❯ **Push your objects into the dough to leave impressions.** Remove the objects and let the dough dry for a few days.

❯ **Closely examine your impressions with a magnifying glass.** What kinds of details can you observe? What do your fossils tell you about the objects that made them? Record your observations in your science journal.

Try This!

Next time you are outside in the rain, try to leave a muddy footprint or shoeprint in your yard. Once the rain stops and the sunshine returns, see if it has hardened. This is how we are able to find dinosaur footprints today. They were walking around in muddy areas and left their footprints in the mud.

SOIL SCIENTIST

CLIMATE KIT
- clear jar with lid
- soil from 3 different locations
- timer

Soil can be found in many locations: your backyard, the bottom of a river, or the bottom of the ocean. It is a mixture of sand, silt, organic material, and clay that comes in all colors and thicknesses. In this experiment, you will be a pedologist. Explore the mixture of things found in soil, investigate the differences between soils from different areas, and look for clues about the surrounding environment.

▶ **Fill a clean, clear jar or bottle** about a third of the way with one kind of soil. What does the soil look like? Record your observations in your science journal.

▶ **Pour water into the jar until it's almost full.** Do you notice any bubbles? What happens to the soil?

▶ **Put the top back on the jar or bottle and shake it vigorously for 20 seconds.** How long do you think it will take before the soil settles? Record your hypothesis in your journal.

▶ **Time how long it takes for the water to turn clear.** Keep in mind that some soils will take days to settle and for the water to turn clear. Record your observations in a chart such as the one below.

Sample #	Time for soil to settle and water to clear	Do layers form? Describe them	Draw what you see
1			
2			
3			

▶ **Repeat with other soil samples.** Try to find soil from unique locations. Why do you think it takes so long for the water to become completely clear? What kind of soil settles the quickest? The slowest? What does this mean for rivers, ponds, and oceans?

Try This!

Next time you are at the beach or lake, bring jars with you to reproduce this experiment. Record your results and compare them with previous experiments.

WORDS TO KNOW

silt: particles of fine soil, rich in nutrients.

pedologist: a scientist who studies soil.

CORE SAMPLING

> **CLIMATE KIT**
> ° vanilla cupcake mix or ingredients
> ° food coloring
> ° clear plastic straws
> ° drawing materials

Scientists use core sampling to study what lies beneath the surface. They take core samples of ice, coral, trees, mud, and rock. In this activity, you will extract and examine core samples from food.

▶ **With a friend or parent,** prepare vanilla cupcakes according to the package directions—only with a twist. Mix up the batter and divide it between three or more bowls. Use food coloring to make a different color of batter in each of the bowls.

▶ **Layer the batter of different colors in the muffin cups.** If possible, layer in different thicknesses, varying the order and thicknesses in each cupcake. Bake the cupcakes according to the instructions.

▶ **While you wait, write down in your journal your predictions** for what your core samples will look like. Which colors will be thicker and which will be thinner?

▶ **Once your cupcakes are out of the oven and cool,** push a clear plastic straw into a cupcake. Rotate the straw through the cupcake as you push down and then pull out. This will help you pull out the core sample.

▶ **What colors are in your core sample?** Was it hard to pull out your core? Make a drawing of what your sample looks like. Take a sample from each cupcake and observe the differences.

A core sample from bedrock in Ontario, Canada
Credit: James St. John (CC BY 2.0)

Try This!

Are there other foods that you can take core samples from? Do you need to use a different tool or technique? What kinds of problems do you encounter when taking a core sample? Think about how hard it might be to pull a core from the ice. What instruments might scientists need to use? How do scientists preserve ice cores to keep them from melting?

OCEAN ACIDIFICATION

Our oceans are becoming more acidic. The **pH** of a liquid is measured on a scale of 0 to 14 and it tells us if a liquid is acidic. A pH of less than 7 is acidic. A pH of greater than 7 is **basic**. Pure water has a pH of 7. The further a liquid's pH is from the number 7, the more acidic or basic it is. The most acidic liquid in the world has a pH of 0. Most organisms that live in the water need a pH range between 6 to 8.

> **CLIMATE KIT**
> ° small cups
> ° various liquid substances to test from the chart on the next page
> ° litmus paper from a hardware store or aquarium supply store

▶ **Start a scientific method worksheet in your science journal.** Create a chart like the one on the following page to record your observations.

▶ **Make a prediction about what the pH of common household** substances will be. Remember, a pH of less than 7 is an acid, more than 7 is a base. Use your chart to record your predictions.

▶ **Pour small amounts of each substance into the cups.** Dip your **litmus paper** into each cup and record the results for each substance. Compare the results to your predictions.

Try This!

Make a new data table and make predictions of what the pH will be when you mix substances together. Only use the items from this list. Do not use strong acids or bases, because they are dangerous. Do not use bleach.

WORDS TO KNOW

pH: a measure of acidity or alkalinity, on a scale from 0 (most acidic) to 14 (most basic).

basic: describes a substance with a bitter taste that often feels slippery. Soap is usually a base. So is baking soda and ammonia.

litmus paper: a special paper used to test whether a substance is an acid or a base.

Substance	Your Prediction	pH (litmus paper)
distilled water		
tap water		
rainwater		
soda water		
soapy water		
baking soda (mix with distilled water)		
aspirin (crush one pill and mix with 4 teaspoons of distilled water)		
tomato juice		
orange juice		
vinegar		
white milk		
chocolate milk		

Take It Further

The oceans are absorbing as much as half of the CO_2 emitted by burning fossil fuels. The more CO_2 the oceans absorb, the more acidic seawater will become, lowering the pH of the world's oceans. Organisms such as gastropods, bivalves, corals, and some plankton have shells or skeletons made of calcium carbonate, which is affected by this increase in acidity. See for yourself what happens when a shell is exposed to acid by putting a seashell in vinegar.

Chapter 5

EARTH HAS A
FEVER

Have you heard news stories about the warming temperature of the planet? Earth is now 2.1 degrees Fahrenheit (1.2 degrees Celsius) degrees warmer on average than it was in 1850. And while 2 degrees might sound like a small difference, it is having a great impact on the world's climate. The change is also affecting everything from endangered species to food production.

ESSENTIAL QUESTION

How is human activity warming the planet?

Plus, in some places, the earth is much, much warmer than just 2 degrees. Some regions within the Arctic have warmed the most rapidly, with Alaska and western Canada's temperature rising between 5.4 and 7.2 degrees Fahrenheit.

EARTH HAS A FEVER

Scientists have been recording Earth's global temperature for more than 130 years, since 1880. They use this temperature data to analyze and make conclusions about the health of the planet. Their conclusion is that Earth has a fever.

Have you ever had a fever? What did it feel like? You probably had your temperature taken and got some medicine. Maybe you went to the doctor.

We call Earth's fever "climate change." Earth's rising temperature has been observed and recorded all around the globe, from deserts to glaciers, from mountaintops to ocean waters.

How did Earth get a fever? Human activity. About 99 percent of scientists agree that humans and human activities are the reason for climate change.

WORDS TO KNOW

endangered: a plant or animal with a very low population that is at risk of disappearing entirely.

climatologist: a scientist who studies the climate.

Humans have been recording **TEMPERATURE** since Galileo's time. The first **THERMOMETERS** were invented during the early 1700s. Classical thermometers use materials such as alcohol or mercury that change volume when heated or cooled. Most of today's thermometers are digital.

Fever Map

One of the easiest ways to check temperature changes through history and today is to read thermometers. **Climatologists** have used thermometers and weather stations in many places, such as Antarctica, Europe, Hawaii, and the North Pole, to record temperatures since the 1880s. To display the increase in global temperatures, NASA uses a heat map. A heat map uses colors from blue to red to represent changes in temperature. What does the color red indicate?

Check out this progressive heat map from NASA that uses data from 1880 to 2018. What do you see happening?

🔍 NASA global warming 2018

CLIMATE CHANGE

Smoke from a factory made it hard to see in this Ohio town, 1973. But the Clean Air Act, passed in 1970, made a big difference!
Credit: Environmental Protection Agency

EARTH'S FEVER

For the past 351 months—almost 30 years—global temperatures have been above the twentieth-century average. The fossil record, ice, coral reefs, mud, and tree rings all provide information about our past climate, which we can compare to our current climate.

We have evidence that human activities are impacting our climate at an alarming rate. Scientific organizations around the world have issued public statements supporting this conclusion and warning people about the consequences of continuing in this way. Most governments around the world are passing laws and initiatives to help curb the kinds of activities that lead to climate change.

As the world's population grows, the demand for energy increases. Burning more and more fossil fuels to power our lives makes Earth's fever worse! Do you use a computer, phone, tablet, or television? These devices require energy. It takes energy to make electronic devices and it takes energy to run them. Fossil fuels produce this energy, but burning them also releases greenhouse gases into the atmosphere. These greenhouse gases cause our Earth to heat up.

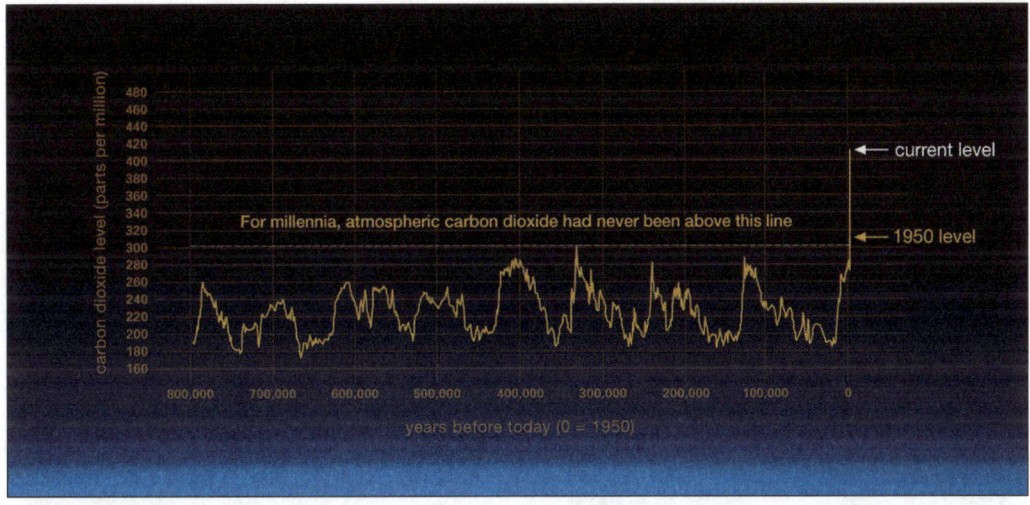

This graph shows how much the level of CO_2 in the atmosphere has increased since ancient times. Scientists used ice core samples to determine the levels before written records.
Credit: NASA

This graph shows a dramatic increase in CO_2 levels beginning in the 1900s. Why do you think that is? Cars and electricity both became more widely used in the United States in the early 1900s. The graph shows us that as our demand for energy from fossil fuels has increased, so too has the amount of CO_2 in the atmosphere.

Our increased need for energy means that we burn more fossil fuels, which adds more CO_2 to the atmosphere. Remember what happens when we add too much CO_2 to the atmosphere? Earth heats up, which affects many of its different systems.

Paris Agreement

On November 4, 2016, almost every country in the world joined in a historic agreement to strengthen the global response to the threat of climate change. The meeting took place in Paris and is known as the Paris Agreement. The meeting's aim was to get worldwide commitment from all nations to take ambitious efforts to combat climate change and adapt to its effects, with enhanced support to assist developing countries to do so.

Sadly, on June 1, 2017, President Donald Trump pulled the United States out of the Paris Agreement.

CLIMATE CHANGE

> **WORDS TO KNOW**
>
> **consumption:** the use of a resource.
>
> **BCE:** put after a date, BCE stands for Before Common Era and counts down to zero. CE stands for Common Era and counts up from zero. This book was printed in 2020 CE.

DINNER!

The use of electronic devices isn't the only thing contributing to the warming of the planet. Take a look in your kitchen to find more ways human lifestyles help heat the planet.

Meat has more of an impact on the environment than any other food. As we learned in Chapter 3, methane contributes to global warming. Drilling and mining for fossil fuels are the leading human activities that produce methane. Another leading cause of methane is the large-scale production of cows, sheep, goats, pigs, and chickens.

Why are we growing and eating all these animals? Because many of us like to eat meat! It is a source of protein and our bodies need protein. But that **consumption** of meat is impacting our climate.

Bacon is one of the oldest meats in history. The Chinese were preserving pork by 1500 **BCE**!

BEEF requires **20 TIMES** more **LAND** and emits **20 TIMES** more greenhouse gas **EMISSIONS** per gram of edible protein than **COMMON PLANT** proteins, such as beans.

EARTH HAS A FEVER

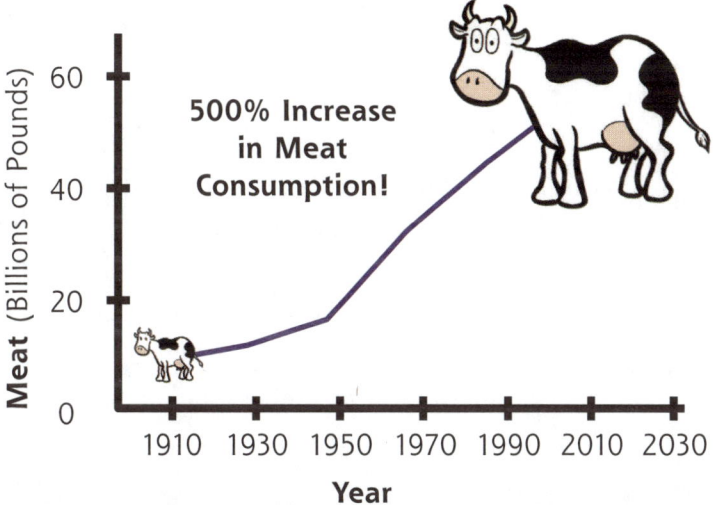

This graph shows that we have been increasing our consumption of meat in the United States since the early 1900s. U.S. consumption has increased 500 percent in the last century. The average American adult eats 222.2 pounds of red meat and poultry in a year! How does this affect our environment?

The environmental costs of eating meat produced by industrial farms are significant. Think about a hamburger. How much energy and how many resources did it take to get that hamburger on your plate? The sun grew the grass that the cow ate. Water fed that grass and the cow. Fuel was used to transport the meat from the farm to the meat-packing plant to your grocery store, and then from the grocery store to your home. That is a lot of resources for one hamburger. It takes a lot more energy to produce a pound of meat than it does to produce a pound of vegetables.

Small, local farms are often more environmentally conscious of the impact they have on the climate.

Animals raised for meat are environmentally troublesome for other reasons, too. When we make lots of animals live together in a small area, we concentrate their waste products, which can pollute the water and air.

A third of all CROPS on the planet go to FEEDING ANIMALS. Two-thirds of all the WATER used on the planet is used for AGRICULTURE. One hamburger requires about 53 gallons of water to get to your plate!

CLIMATE CHANGE

WORDS TO KNOW

reflect: to bounce off a surface. To redirect something that hits a surface, such as heat, light, or sound.

absorb: to soak up a liquid or take in energy, heat, light, or sound.

black carbon: the sooty black material emitted from gas and diesel engines, coal-fired power plants, and other sources that burn fossil fuels.

A BALLOONING POPULATION

When looking at energy data, it's important to remember that the human population was 1 billion in 1800. Since then, the human population has risen to 7.8 billion. All of these people need food, as well as energy to cook food, build and light homes and businesses, recharge electronics, fuel cars, and power factories.

It takes **20 POUNDS** of **CROPS** to produce just **ONE POUND** of meat!

The world population releases about 2.57 million pounds of CO_2 into the air every second. There are 86,400 seconds in a single day, which means humans release 222 billion pounds of CO_2 into the atmosphere every day. All this excess CO_2 is what drives the changes in our climate.

How Big Is Your Footprint?

The human activities—from using technology to transportation—that we perform every day release CO_2 into the atmosphere. As the world's population continues to grow, it is important to understand our personal and community carbon footprints. A carbon footprint is the measure of the amount of greenhouse gases that are produced directly or indirectly from your activities. Your personal carbon footprint takes into account the food you eat, your transportation methods, how you heat your home, and how much electricity you use. This footprint is measured in equivalent tons of CO_2.

With an adult's help, you can figure out the size of your carbon footprint at this website. What can you do to reduce that footprint?

🔍 EPA footprint calculator

EARTH HAS A FEVER

Since the United States was founded in 1776, our use of energy has been increasing. In fact, in the United States, our primary energy production comes from the three major fossil fuels—petroleum, natural gas, and coal. Our use of renewable energy, mainly from hydropower (water), wind, and solar, has been increasing since the 1990s. To help combat the climate crisis, we need to increase this use of renewable energies even more.

Black Carbon

Glaciers have a bright, white surface, which means they **reflect** most of the sunlight hitting them instead of **absorbing** it. This helps keep temperatures in the polar regions cool. But burning fossil fuels creates **black carbon**, which settles as a visible layer of black soot on the glaciers. When that happens, glaciers absorb more sunlight and melt more quickly. How does this impact the water level of the world's oceans? What happens to animals that live on the ice? How could this contribute to Earth's rising temperature? Black carbon also has many negative impacts on human health. Breathing in black carbon causes health problems, such as respiratory and cardiovascular disease, cancer, and even birth defects.

CLIMATE CHANGE

> **WORDS TO KNOW**
>
> **deforestation:** the process through which forests are cleared to use land for other purposes.

One yellow school bus weighs 10,000 pounds. Americans release the weight of more than 700,000 school buses of CO_2 into our atmosphere from transportation— EVERY DAY.

WHAT IS PROGRESS?

Not so long ago, the United States generated most of its electricity from renewable resources. The early settlers burned biofuel in the form of trees, corn cob husks, and other materials. They also learned how to harness the wind and water and used windmills and watermills to power simple machines.

For thousands of years, humans relied on the energy from renewable sources for all of their cooking, heating, and lighting needs. When and why did humankind become so dependent on nonrenewable fossil fuels?

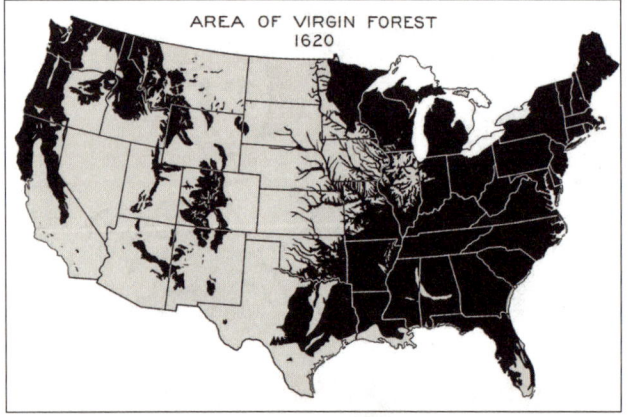
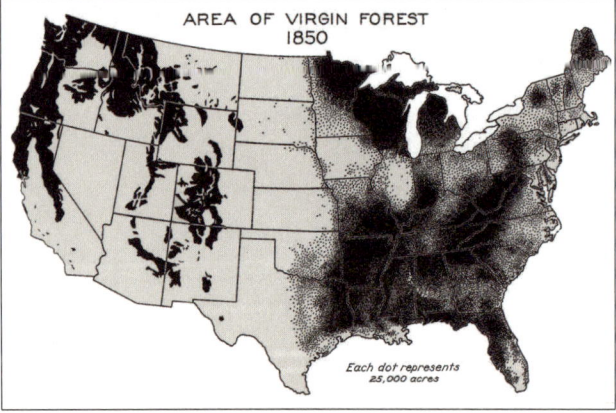
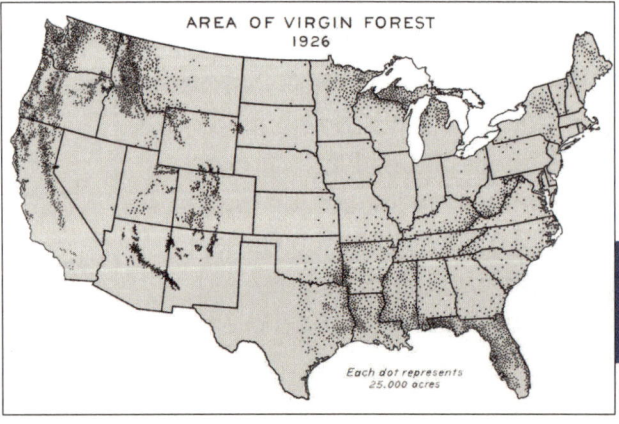

These maps show the progress of deforestation in the United States during the past 400 years.

Warren Washington

Warren Washington (1936–) holds a Ph.D. in meteorology and is a leading expert in climate research. Using computer models, he has identified patterns and made predictions about greenhouse gases and temperatures for the future. His computer models help identify relationships between activities such as burning fossil fuels and climate change.

Wood was once a bountiful source of heat and light across the country. A growing population used so much wood from forests to power their lives, cook their food, and build their homes that the result was massive **deforestation**. The need for land to raise crops and livestock was another major factor contributing to the loss of forests. While the United States hasn't returned to its previous levels of forest coverage, fewer trees are being cut down every year to satisfy energy needs.

Train hoppers filled with coal, 1974

CLIMATE CHANGE

WORDS TO KNOW

extinct: when a species completely dies out.

industrialization: the widespread development of manufacturing, with products made by machines in large factories.

Partly this is because of conservation efforts to save and restore the forests. Partly it's because humans found the energy they needed from other resources.

During the first half of the 1800s, coal was burned to boil water, which created steam power for trains and boats. Coal became the main energy resource for transportation. In the 1880s, coal was first used to generate electricity for homes and factories. Today, coal is the second-largest source of electricity in the United States and around the world.

Around the same time we began using coal to power our trains and boats, we were using a massive amount of whale oil to light our homes. Whale oil became popular in the 1700s because it burned brighter and had less of a stinky odor than other types of oils. But the whale population suffered because of human energy needs. In fact, whales became an endangered species, at risk of becoming **extinct**.

On August 27, 1859, for the first time in human history, oil was tapped at its source in a field in Titusville, Pennsylvania. This was the very first step toward the large-scale production and use of oil to heat and light our homes and, eventually, to power our cars and airplanes.

The first commercial oil well

84

EARTH HAS A FEVER

Moms Clean Air Force

Our strongest leaders and advocates for families may be this community of more than 1 million moms and dads fighting air pollution! This community network provides information and tools and sponsors events to help protect the health of our communities by fighting for clean air. From the city level to state level, these moms and dads are working to create solutions to the problem of air pollution.

Moms Clean Air Force helps you think globally and act locally. By joining your voice of concern with others in your region, you are able to have more impact locally. According to the World Health Organization (WHO), the combined effects of ambient (outdoor) and household air pollution cause about 7 million premature deaths every year.

Using oil as an energy source allowed for rapid **industrialization**. Oil powered the twentieth century and created the modern world as we know it. Just as the discovery of coal helped save the forests, the discovery of oil helped saved the whale.

The history of our country is one of progress and energy transitions. We have changed how we power our lives through time, from renewables (wood, water, and wind) to fossil fuels (coal, natural gas, and petroleum). Our energy choices shape our society, climate, and our future. By understanding our energy use, we can answer questions, solve problems, and take actions that will reduce our CO_2 emissions.

ESSENTIAL QUESTION

How is human activity warming the planet?

Will we transform into a world powered by energy from renewable sources or will we remain reliant on fossil fuels? Will we continue to release trillions of pounds of methane into the atmosphere or will we adapt to the climate we've created and make headway in righting our mistakes? It's time to seek solutions and learn the value of thinking globally and acting locally. Read the next chapter to see how you can be part of the solution!

MEASURE AIR POLLUTANTS

CLIMATE KIT
- index cards
- petroleum jelly

How do we know what's in the air? Many things are in the air, including pollen, dust, germs, and gases. Dirty air that is full of **pollutants** is called polluted air. Air pollution is one of the consequences of burning fossil fuels. Learn how to test the air and collect and analyze data with this experiment.

▶ **Brainstorm three to five places to test for air pollution.** Some ideas include your bedroom, the refrigerator, or your mailbox. Start a scientific method worksheet in your science journal and record your predictions for which areas you think are most impacted by air pollution.

▶ **Label an index card for each area.** Smear a layer of petroleum jelly in the middle of the index cards and tape each card to its location.

▶ **Check your cards every two days for six days.** In your science journal, record your observations from each location using a chart to keep track of your data.

▶ **Which location had the most air pollution?** Why? What could you do to improve the quality of the air in that area?

Try This!

This experiment explored visible air pollution, but what types of pollution may be invisible to our eyes? Is CO_2 a pollutant? Is CO_2 visible? Some of the worst air pollution in the world exists in China. With an adult's permission, use the internet to find images of this country. What does it look like? Can you see the air pollution? How are people trying to keep themselves healthy?

Types of Pollution

There are other types of pollution, in addition to air pollution. Which of these can you find where you live?

› Water pollution
› Soil pollution
› Light pollution
› Noise pollution

WORDS TO KNOW

pollutant: a substance that is harmful to the environment.

PERFORM A TRANSPORTATION
ENERGY AUDIT

We all use transportation—cars, bikes, trains, buses, airplanes, and our own bodies. Burning 1 gallon of gasoline releases 20 pounds of carbon dioxide into the atmosphere. In the United States, we use 380,000,000 gallons of oil and gas every day for transportation. How much energy does your family use for transportation? How much carbon dioxide does your family release?

An easy way to reduce your **CARBON FOOTPRINT** is not to fly. Airplanes and flying leave a big mark in terms of carbon.

❯ **Ask an adult how many gallons of gas** your family uses in one week for transportation. Record this amount in your science journal.

❯ **Based on your family's weekly use,** how many gallons does your family use each year? One year has 52 weeks. Multiply your weekly use by 52 to get the gallons of gas used in one year.

weekly gas usage × 52 weeks = yearly gas usage

Multiply your yearly use by 20 pounds. This is your family's carbon dioxide emission, or the amount released, for transportation.

yearly gas usage × 20 pounds = CO_2 emissions per year

❯ **In your science journal,** brainstorm ways to reduce your transportation CO_2 emissions. Could you sometimes ride your bike or walk? Do you ever ride the bus or subway? Do you carpool?

Try This!

Identify other activities that use energy. Audit your consumption of meat, hours of light bulbs turned on in your room, or hours spent charging electronic devices. Which behaviors can you change?

LIGHT OVER TIME

CLIMATE KIT
- something to read
- candle
- overhead light
- flashlight

One of the most obvious uses for energy is light. What would your life be like without light? Would you go to bed earlier? Would you be able to read as many books? During human history, we've searched for better and better ways to provide ourselves with light. Let's compare and contrast light from different sources. As you observe the quality of each light, think about points in history when electricity and light bulbs did not exist.

Caution: Have an adult help you with the candle!

▸ **Make a table in your science journal** listing all the light sources. Start a scientific method worksheet and make predictions about the quality of each source of light.

▸ **When it's dark, have an adult light a candle.** Read a couple of pages from a book or magazine using the candlelight. Write down your experience using this type of light. Would you want to use it again?

▸ **Read your book using an overhead light or flashlight.** What do you think of these sources of light? Record your observations.

The Speed of Light

Nothing can travel faster than light. The speed of light in a vacuum is 186,282 miles per second or 670,616,629 miles per hour. If you could travel at the speed of light, you could go around the earth 7.5 times in one second or 27,000 times in one hour. The universe is so large scientists measure distances by how far light travels in one year. For example, the closest stars to our star is Alpha Centauri A and B, which are 4.3 light-years away.

Think About It!

Which was the best type of light to read by? Were any of the lights hard to read with? Can light be good both for the environment and for your eyes?

CARBON
IN THE AIR

CLIMATE KIT
° glass plate
° matches

When wood, coal, natural gas, or oil are burned, CO_2 is released into the air. Carbon dioxide is a colorless and odorless gas, so what proof is there of its release? In this experiment, you will burn a match to see if we can provide visual evidence of the release of carbon. What if we could see all the carbon that we release into the air every day?

Caution: This activity requires the help of an adult.

▶ **Start a scientific method worksheet** in your science journal. What will happen when you hold a burning match under a glass plate?

▶ **Place the glass plate on the counter** so that the plate hangs over the edge of the counter by 2 or 3 inches.

▶ **With an adult, light the match** and hold it under the edge of the plate for a few seconds before blowing it out. Can you see or smell anything on the spot where you held the burning match? Record your observations.

▶ **Once the plate has cooled,** touch the area where you held the match. What does it feel like? Record your observations.

Think About It!

The next time you roast marshmallows around a campfire, notice what happens to the wood as it burns. What does your marshmallow look like if it catches fire? When the campfire is out, what do the bits of burned wood look like? What do you know about the burned parts of the marshmallow and the wood?

Chapter 6

DECIDE THE FUTURE OF
PLANET EARTH

Life on Spaceship Earth is constantly changing. What was the planet like 10,000 years ago? The **Ice Age** was ending and humans lived a **nomadic** life, moving constantly in search of animals to hunt and plants to gather. As our climate warmed up, we **adapted**. We learned to grow food and raise animals. We changed from hunting and gathering to a society based on agriculture.

ESSENTIAL QUESTION

How can we help support the health of planet Earth?

Fast forward to the 1700s and the beginning of the Industrial Revolution. This is when many people moved from agriculture to **industry** and traded farms and forests for factories. All these changes altered our relationship to the natural world.

DECIDE THE FUTURE OF PLANET EARTH

As humanity develops and uses more and more technology to complete everyday tasks—such as machines for washing and drying our clothes and dishes or robots to vacuum our floors—our demand for energy increases. The demand for energy is 25 times greater today than it was 100 years ago.

Our shifting world has increased our energy demand in such a short period of time that it has resulted in major changes to wildlife, habitats, and the health of humans. We changed our world so rapidly in the search for cheap energy that we have disrupted ecosystems, the atmosphere, and the health of the planet.

> **WORDS TO KNOW**
>
> **Ice Age:** a period of time when ice covered a large part of Earth.
> **nomadic:** moving from place to place to find food and water.
> **adapt:** to change to survive in new or different conditions.
> **industry:** the large-scale production of goods, especially in factories.

The United States has only 4.4 PERCENT of the world's population, but contributes 15 PERCENT of the world's CARBON EMISSIONS.

The Industrial Revolution led to more people living in cities.

CLIMATE CHANGE

WORDS TO KNOW

iteration: using a process that repeats itself, such as developing a game, testing it, developing it further, and testing it again.

ingenuity: the ability to solve difficult problems creatively.

innovation: a new creation or a unique solution to a problem.

efficient: wasting as little energy as possible.

conserve: to save or protect something, or to use it carefully so it isn't used up.

wind farm: groups or clusters of wind turbines that produce large amounts of electricity together.

Giants of Science

U.S. President Barack Obama (1961–) led the first **iteration** of the Climate Action Plan in June 2013 to commit the United States to reducing carbon emissions. The United States is the second-largest producer of carbon dioxide in the world, behind China. Part of the Climate Action Plan focuses on getting companies to reduce carbon emissions. Reducing carbon emissions is essential to addressing climate change.

Like the Great Wall of China, AIR POLLUTION is often VISIBLE FROM SPACE.

All of this might sound hopeless, but we still have time to heal the negative impacts of our endless search for and burning of fossil fuels. Humans have accomplished many great things, including flight, walking on the moon, and finding cures for terrible diseases. Through **ingenuity** and **innovation**, we have shaped the present, and now we must use that same ingenuity to shape the future.

Nothing's Perfect

Alternative energy sources, including renewable energies, have trade-offs. So far, we haven't found an energy source that is perfect. Every source of energy has an impact on our environment, from the dangerous radioactive waste of nuclear power to the interruption in animal and plant habitats that can result from the building of dams. What's the solution? Educating ourselves and pushing the boundaries of research to continue improving our energy use and reducing the human impact on the planet.

We are all responsible for making positive changes to keep Spaceship Earth a healthy place to live.

ENERGY INVENTIONS

How do we use energy on Spaceship Earth? What do we use to light our homes, cook our food, and power our electronics? Could we be more **efficient** in our use of energy?

Human civilization is full of inventions, from railroads that connect the East and West Coasts to the internet that connects people all over the world. Many inventions relate to energy and how we use it.

A floating wind farm
Credit: Martin Pettitt (CC BY 2.0)

As we understand more about the human impact on climate change, we can use our ingenuity to invent products that **conserve** energy.

People have designed batteries that enable cars to run on electricity instead of gasoline, which is healthier for the environment. Engineers have built floating solar panels to better harvest the energy of the sun to power our cities. Have you ever heard of **wind farms**? Instead of vegetables, wind farms produce electricity by harnessing energy that blows naturally.

CLIMATE CHANGE

WORDS TO KNOW

photovoltaic (PV): able to produce electricity from sunlight.

hydrokinetic: relating to the motion of fluids.

galvanize: to shock or excite someone into taking action.

What is the difference between EFFICIENCY and CONSERVATION?

The U.S. armed forces are using renewable energy to power bases abroad and military communities at home. Today, nearly 31 states and the District of Columbia are using solar **photovoltaic (PV)** energy systems at Navy, Army, and Air Force bases. The armed forces are a leader of renewable power generation, nearly doubling it between 2011 and 2015 and creating enough power for about 286,000 average U.S. homes.

What powers your classroom? More than 5,000 schools in the United States currently have solar panels that collect energy from the sun and use it to keep classrooms bright and warm. Maybe your school will be next!

Take a look at some of the ways people are using marine and **hydrokinetic** technologies to harvest the energy of the oceans!

🔍 hydrokinetic energy video

This solar array at High Desert Montessori Charter School in Reno, Nevada, will save the school about $30,000 a year on its utility bill.

Credit: BlackRockSolar (CC BY 2.0)

DECIDE THE FUTURE OF PLANET EARTH

All these inventions were created by people, including kids, who saw the need for new ways of making and using energy. Scientists, engineers, mathematicians, moms, dads, and grandparents have put their heads together to think of and build solutions. Let's explore some of the people designing solutions to address global climate change.

Most Americans search for the term "GLOBAL WARMING" rather than "CLIMATE CHANGE" when searching online for information about our changing climate. Scientists prefer to use climate change because the impacts of climate change vary, depending on the geographic location, habitat, and communities.

"Change Your Ways"

Greta Thunberg (2003–) is a Swedish student leading global awareness and activism against climate change. Her efforts have created a global school strike to hold politicians accountable for their decisions that lead to a worsening climate. She is **galvanizing** the next generation of leaders and activists. In 2019, she won the Ambassador of Conscience Award from Amnesty International. This is a human rights award.

CLIMATE CHANGE

WORDS TO KNOW

engineering: the use of science, math, and creativity to design and build things.

empower: to give someone authority and power.

NEVER TOO YOUNG OR TOO OLD

Kids around the globe are taking positive community actions to protect the air, water, and land on Spaceship Earth. Plus, they're laying their own foundations by learning the science, technology, **engineering**, and math that is crucial for solving the problem of climate change. We can't even imagine the kinds of climate-related jobs there will be 50 years from now, so it's important to gain critical and creative thinking skills to be ready for whatever comes next.

In 2019, a 16-year-old climate activist with Asperger syndrome, **GRETA THUNBERG**, was nominated for the Nobel Peace Prize. Although she didn't win, she did address the United Nations General Assembly and has won many other awards. You can follow Greta on Twitter at @GretaThunberg. In her own words, "**YOU MUST UNITE BEHIND THE SCIENCE. YOU MUST TAKE ACTION. YOU MUST DO THE IMPOSSIBLE. BECAUSE GIVING UP CAN NEVER EVER BE AN OPTION.**"

ACEing It

The Alliance for Climate Education (ACE) is instrumental in bringing the stories of leadership and opportunities to combat climate change to young people. This organization focuses on educating young people about the climate and helping them organize their efforts to act both individually and as members of a larger group in bringing awareness of the problem around the world.

Want to learn more? Check out its website here.

🔍 Alliance for Climate Education

DECIDE THE FUTURE OF PLANET EARTH

For some kids, climate change can be overwhelming. Many feel they can't save the climate alone. Using an annual social media campaign called #Youth4Climate to join the call for climate action is a great way to feel **empowered**. This is a way to connect with a community of kids who share the challenges, concerns, and hopes for a sustainable future.

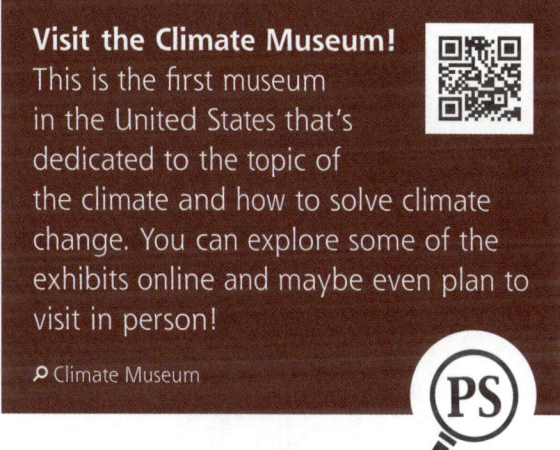

Visit the Climate Museum!
This is the first museum in the United States that's dedicated to the topic of the climate and how to solve climate change. You can explore some of the exhibits online and maybe even plan to visit in person!

🔍 Climate Museum

Campaigning, marching, walking, singing, tweeting, posting, photographing—all these actions are part of The Wild Center's Youth Summits. Organized by The Wild Center and the Association for Science and Technology Centers, these events are hosted by high school students. Each summit brings together kids, activists, parents, scientists, college students, and media to educate and collaborate and produce climate action plans that include actions participants can take to tackle climate change. You can learn more about this program at The Wild Center's website or do some research and find a summit in your area.

Join a climate march!
Credit: julian meehan (CC BY 2.0)

CLIMATE CHANGE

> **WORDS TO KNOW**
>
> **vertical farming:** growing food on vertical surfaces, such as the sides of buildings or skyscrapers.

REINVENTING OUR FUTURE

It may seem like a big challenge to slow climate change, but humans are pretty good at tackling big projects. We sent a robot to Mars! Reimagining and creating new products is an important part of changing everyday behavior and reducing greenhouse gas emissions.

From ELECTRIC CARS to ELECTRIC SCOOTERS, we are engineering transportation that has the potential to run on RENEWABLES!

In London, they are doing just that—implementing a small change to address a big issue. London's famous bright red telephone boxes have fallen out of use because everyone now has cell phones. What do Londoners need instead of public telephones? Charging stations! The city is painting the old red boxes green and adding solar panels to the roofs to create charging stations. Now, you can plug in your cell phone, tablet, camera, or other device and power them from the sun, right on the streets of London.

Making red telephone boxes "go green" is one small way to help slow climate change. And it shows how an outdated invention can be transformed for a new, clean-energy purpose.

Electric Vehicles

The number of electric vehicles on the road is increasing every year. Electric vehicles use electricity for their power. Electric vehicles use batteries, plug-ins, or a combination of batteries and fossil fuels. There are also lots more choices than ever before for electric scooters and bicycles. Can you imagine a day when our transportation by car, bike, bus, or plane will be fully electric?

DECIDE THE FUTURE OF PLANET EARTH

Food is another opportunity for us to change our behaviors. The majority of the food we eat is grown on farms in rural areas. Farms can take up many hundreds and thousands of acres of land and may require specific climates. In a modern world, what invention could we come up with to improve our 12,000-year-old history of farming?

"GOING GREEN" is the term used to describe changes that help IMPROVE our ENVIRONMENT and CLIMATE.

How about **vertical farming**? Vertical farms are just as they sound, crops being grown in stacked layers. These farms produce some of your favorite green vegetables, such as kale and spinach. Vertical farms can be on the sides of buildings in cities such as Singapore or indoors in cold climates. Vertical farms use environmentally friendly techniques to grow food. Some vertical farms recycle water or use special soil to grow foods. From Massachusetts to Dubai, vertical farms are reshaping communities. People learn to grow and eat local food while new jobs are created.

A wall of vertical farms
Credit: State Department photo by Saverio Lombardi Vallauri/ Public Domain

CLIMATE CHANGE

> **WORDS TO KNOW**
>
> **urban farming:** growing or producing food in a city or heavily populated area.
>
> **carbon footprint:** the total amount of carbon dioxide and other greenhouse gases emitted during the full life cycle of a product or service or by a person or family in a year.

The largest indoor vertical farm, at 215,000-square-feet, in the United States is in Las Vegas, Nevada. It uses recycled water and LED lighting to grow crops 365 days a year. Head to the East Coast, in the area of Newark, New Jersey, and you will find a farm where technology and science combine to grow greens using LED lights and a special cloth for soil.

Urban farming is changing the landscape and community of major cities. Urban farmers believe in supporting environmental stewardship and bringing together community members.

In 2006, the city of Detroit, Michigan, had many unused spaces in the form of abandoned lots and homes. Malik Yakini opened one of the city's first urban farms in Detroit on an a tiny, unused plot of land. His goal was to bring more fresh food to members of his community. Today, there are more than 1,400 growing locations in and around the city. Worldwide, an estimated 800 million people participate in urban farming.

Society is taking note of the need to adapt to the changing climate. One significant way to voice your concern for the changing climate is how you spend your money. It's called the power of the purse. Many large institutions are no longer investing in companies that produce fossil fuels. Instead, they are investing in more sustainable companies.

Welcome to Heat Island

Some people call trees "nature's air conditioner" for the cooling shade they provide on warm summer days. In fact, many cities around the world are planting more trees to combat something known as the urban heat island. This is when urban areas experience elevated temperatures compared to their rural surroundings—this difference in temperature is known as an urban heat island. Why do you think cities would be hotter than the surrounding countryside?

A city garden
Credit: Linda (CC BY 2.0)

TREES help our **EARTH**, animals, and humans breathe. Trees absorb our CO_2 and produce **OXYGEN**. One acre of trees produces enough oxygen for 18 people each year. One tree produces nearly 260 pounds of oxygen each year.

The University of California, for example, decided in 2018 to cut any of its $80,000,000 of investments with fossil fuel companies. In fact, your parents or grandparents may have even chosen to move their financial investments to companies that perform more sustainably. Ask your parents if they invest in sustainable companies. What do you spend your allowance on?

There are other actions each and every individual can take to reduce their **carbon footprint** and their impact on our fragile environment. Eating less meat can significantly reduce your carbon footprint. You don't have to give up entirely, but just reducing your consumption of meat can really help. There are also new meat alternatives made from plant protein that taste like meat. Two companies are making lots of news these days with their alternative meats. Have you heard of the Incredible Burger or Beyond Meat?

CLIMATE CHANGE

WORDS TO KNOW

incinerator: a large furnace used to burn trash.

compost: to recycle food scraps and vegetation and put them back in the soil.

CLEANUP ON AISLE EARTH

Another way people are working to slow climate change is by finding better ways to deal with waste. In the United States, most of the garbage goes to landfills or **incinerators**. Both landfills and incinerators contribute to global warming. As garbage rots or is burned, it releases methane, a dangerous gas contributing to climate change. Decaying garbage not only adds greenhouse gases to our atmosphere, it also contributes other harmful pollutants to our air, land, and water.

What else can we do with our garbage? More than 40 percent of the trash we throw away could be recycled. Much of our trash is food waste that could be **composted**. Some towns and businesses around the country are even making composting the rule to help curb climate change. Does your school have a composting program? How does it work?

We could also do a better job disposing of our trash. To help with this, companies are redesigning the way trash cans look and function—using solar energy along with a bin with lever or door. Solar panels are placed on the trash can to harness energy that the bin uses to compact the trash into a far smaller piece of waste. These trash cans help reduce the amount of trash on the streets, at colleges and universities, airports, and in our landfills. Have you spotted a solar-powered trash can?

Pollution greatly affects the world's oceans. The OCEAN is more than just a home to marine species. The ocean absorbs CARBON DIOXIDE from the atmosphere, helping to keep us in BALANCE and playing an important role in slowing CLIMATE CHANGE.

Much of the plastic we throw out never makes it to a landfill, incinerator, or recycling center—it ends up in our oceans. By cleaning up the oceans, especially of plastics, we make it easier for the oceans to support life and absorb carbon dioxide.

One Tree, Two Tree

How many trees have you planted in your life? How many do you think you could plant in one hour? Ethiopia planted more than 353 million trees in 12 hours in July 2019.

This massive tree-planting effort was part of a reforestation campaign named "Green Legacy," started by the country's prime minister, Abiy Ahmed. Millions of Ethiopians across the country were invited to participate in the challenge and showed up to take part in this world record-setting event. Other countries have also had massive tree-planting initiatives. In 2016, India planted 49.3 million trees in a day.

Credit: Trees for the Future (CC BY 2.0)

How does this help the planet? Trees help remove CO_2 from the atmosphere, produce rainfall, and provide homes and food for plants and animals. In fact, there are three species of supertrees that our vital to our environment. These trees are found in Brazil, Indonesia, and the Republic of Congo.

Our oceans and forests are critical to addressing climate change. In fact, Honolulu, a city in Hawaii, banned plastic utensils, food containers, and straws to help protect its beautiful waters. Other cities around the world have followed suit in an effort to reduce the amount of plastic finding its way to the oceans.

CLIMATE CHANGE

WORDS TO KNOW

STEM: an acronym that stands for science, technology, engineering, and mathematics. STEAM is STEM plus art.

CAREERS THAT SHAPE OUR PLANET

Have you ever heard of the term "green jobs"? It refers to jobs that help protect our environment and our earth. Many of these green jobs involve subjects such as science, technology, engineering, math, and art. You might have heard these subjects called the **STEM** or STEAM subjects.

The world needs kids such as you to get involved as scientists, engineers, designers, and inventors. Many different jobs are involved in studying and slowing climate change.

Here's a list of energy and STEAM careers related to the climate. Work with a parent to research these jobs online:

- oceanographer
- meteorologist
- ecologist
- geologist
- green building contractor
- home energy auditor
- climate change researcher
- air quality specialist
- climate program officer
- climate change community organizer
- sustainable development director
- carbon management consultant

Watch this video to get inspired. Explore how these students from across the country are helping their schools and communities go green. The Green Ambassadors program works with students and teachers to implement green changes.

🔍 young voices ambassadors

DECIDE THE FUTURE OF PLANET EARTH

Greening Your School

Students across the country are teaming up to shrink the carbon footprints of their schools. Some of the following steps are local actions you can take to reduce your energy use and decrease greenhouse gas emissions.

- ❏ Recycling: No need to fill up our landfills with cans, bottles, and paper! Recycle everything possible.

- ❏ Composting: When you don't eat that broccoli or peanut butter and jelly sandwich, do you throw it in the trash? Ask your school to start composting. Putting food waste in the form of compost back into the soil helps replenish nutrients.

- ❏ School garden: Once you start composting, have your school or classroom plant a garden. The garden can help you learn about energy and even grow food for school lunches.

- ❏ Trees: Did you know that planting trees is one of the easiest ways to help clean our air and fight climate change? You can plant trees in your school's playground and outside areas. One tree can absorb nearly 1 ton of CO_2 in its lifetime.

- ❏ Energy-efficient lighting: Many schools still use old fluorescent light bulbs that are less efficient than newly designed light bulbs. Research what light bulbs are used in your school. Create a campaign for your school to change the light bulbs to more efficient ones.

- ❏ Water-efficient bathroom sinks and toilets: Each student in your school goes to the bathroom at least once a day. That uses a lot of water. Start a campaign to have automatic water sinks and toilets installed so you can reduce the amount of water used.

- ❏ Large windows: One easy way to help conserve energy is to make sure that classrooms and common spaces get daylight so lights don't need to be turned on.

- ❏ Smart thermostats: These can show the actual temperature in your classroom and help regulate temperatures in your school. They can also work on timers so the heat or air conditioning isn't on during the evenings or weekends.

- ❏ Use of paper: In your classroom, use both sides of the paper when printing or writing. Use scrap paper for art projects and practice work.

CLIMATE CHANGE

WORDS TO KNOW

citizen science: the involvement of everyday people in scientific activities or projects.

If you're not a scientist yet but want to help track the impact of climate change, you can find **citizen science** projects to become involved in. These are projects done by local people to help scientists gather and analyze data. Many of these projects involve making observations or collecting data.

What happens in one part of the globe affects other locations. When a volcano erupts in Iceland, the ash disrupts airplanes across Europe. Warming waters in the Indian Ocean change the fishing off the coast of Africa. Citizen scientists play a large role in collecting data from all around the globe to help us understand what is happening. From tracking bird migration to taking pictures underwater, these projects help scientists solve problems.

Human activity is changing our PLANET. Are we making changes to improve, maintain, and care for the systems that SUPPORT LIFE on SPACESHIP EARTH? Or are we damaging the very systems that we rely on for our EXISTENCE?

Citizen Science: Counting Birds

The Great Backyard Bird Count, hosted by the Cornell Lab of Ornithology and National Audubon Society, is an annual project that examines birds. Bird migration can tell us a lot about climate change. As temperatures get warmer, migration patterns change. The data gathered by ordinary citizens during a four-day count helps scientists better understand the impacts of climate change. Why is citizen science important? How can regular people contribute to the growing collection of knowledge about climate change?

DECIDE THE FUTURE OF PLANET EARTH

Credit: NPS Climate Change Response

What is Bioplastic?

Bioplastic is made from fish scales and red algae. It was invented by Lucy Hughes of the University of Sussex in England. She wanted to invent something that would be compostable. Her invention, called MarinaTex, is a filmlike plastic wrap meant for one-time use. This film can be composted at home in just four to six weeks. A perfect invention to wrap up those leftovers!

CLIMATE CHANGE

The Climate March in Washington, DC, 2017
Credit: Mark Dixon (CC BY 2.0)

American scientist Margaret Mead (1901–1978) once said, "Never doubt that a small group of thoughtful, committed citizens can change the world; indeed, it's the only thing that ever has." What do you think she meant?

Think globally about how we are impacting our planet with our choices and act locally to be part of the solution.

PBS *SciGirls* is a new show for kids ages 8 to 12 years old that shares the stories of bright, curious, real tween girls putting science, technology, engineering, and math (STEM) to work in their everyday lives. In each half-hour episode, you'll meet a new group of girls!

🔎 PBSkids SciGirls

ESSENTIAL QUESTION

How can we help support the health of planet Earth?

108

PLANT TREES IN
YOUR COMMUNITY

CLIMATE KIT
- recycled material for fliers
- drawing materials
- seeds or a tree

You've learned in this book that plants are critical to the balance of gases in our atmosphere because they absorb carbon dioxide and release oxygen. Planting a tree is an easy and important part of fighting climate change. With your family and friends, organize a campaign to plant trees in your neighborhood!

❯ **Create a flyer about planting trees** in your neighborhood or school using markers or crayons and recycled materials. Include some of the facts you have learned about global warming. List some of the other benefits trees provide—shade, climbing opportunities, and beauty. Encourage people to become part of the solution!

❯ **With an adult's permission,** go online to research what types of trees grow best in your region. What type of soil do different trees need to thrive? Does it get very cold in the winter? How long is your growing season? Be sure to give your trees the best possible start by choosing the right varieties.

Not only are **TREES** a necessary part of maintaining **BALANCE** in the **ATMOSPHERE**, they contribute to the **BIODIVERSITY** of other species. Research has shown that adding one tree to an open pasture can increase its bird biodiversity from almost zero species to as many as 80.

❯ **With an adult, order your 10 free trees** from the Arbor Foundation or purchase trees from a local arbor or gardening center.

❯ **In your science journal, make a record** of when and where you plant the trees. Come up with a plan to care for them as they grow. Trees need regular watering during the first year after planting.

Try This!

Track the growth of the new trees. Measure their height and width every month and record the measurements in your science journal. Are some trees growing faster than others? Why? Is the soil different? Are they getting more or less sun? Track the growth during a year and share your results with the people who helped you plant the trees. How big do you think they'll be in five years? Ten years?

WRITE A LETTER TO THE
MAYOR OR THE GOVERNOR

Every day, our government officials at both the state and national levels make decisions that impact climate change. Make sure your voice is heard!

▶ **Ask an adult to help you find the name and address** of a local or state elected official. You can usually find this information online. A mayor is a government official who leads a city or town. If your town doesn't have a mayor, write to your governor, who is the leader of your state. Write the name and address on the envelope.

▶ **Make a list in your science journal of the points** you want to include in your letter. What commitments can you make to help stop climate change? What information about climate change can you share with the elected official? What do you want the mayor to do?

▶ **Draft your letter.** Note that elected officials appreciate and respond to original letters. If you need help writing your letter, look at the sample language on the next page as a starting point.

▶ **Revise your letter.** Make sure you use correct grammar and spelling! Have a parent read your letter and revise it again if necessary.

▶ **Fold your letter neatly and put it in the envelope.** Put a stamp on it and send it off in the mail.

Write Away!

Don't stop by simply writing a letter to your local official. You can write a letter to your U.S. senator and representative and even the president of the United States. Tell the president what you would like them to do to combat climate change.

The White House
1600 Pennsylvania Avenue NW
Washington, DC 20500

Dear Mayor _____,

I am writing to let you know that I have learned about climate change and want to help. I recently read *Climate Change: The Science Behind Melting Glaciers and Warming Oceans* by Joshua Sneideman and Erin Twamley and realize that climate change is impacting my home, my friends, and our community. Climate change is impacting me because _____. I have committed to helping stop climate change by _____.

I am writing to you to ask for your help. I would like you to consider signing the U.S. Mayors Climate Protection Agreement that has been signed by nearly 400 of your colleagues. It's a 12-step program that sets reasonable goals for our city to reduce carbon dioxide emissions to below what the levels were in 1990.

Please join these other mayors in being leaders in the fight to stop climate change. The kids of the world are depending on you.

Sincerely,

_____, Age ____

Try This!

Research other organizations that officials can join or sign a pledge of support for. Write to other government leaders encouraging them to show support for slowing climate change.

TRACK YOUR
WASTE

Do you know how much food you waste in a day? Our food waste contributes to climate change. The production of food requires the use of energy. When we throw away food, we are wasting energy and food. How can you change your behaviors to help reduce waste? Try this activity for a day or a week and find out.

❱ **Start a scientific method worksheet** in your science journal. Create a Waste Tracking Chart. How much food does your family waste each week?

❱ **After every meal or snack, record what you don't eat** and don't plan to eat as leftovers. Write down how much food you wasted and how you threw it away. Did it go in the trash? The compost bin? Did you feed it to the dog under the table? Ask an adult to help you estimate the cost of the wasted food.

❱ **At the end of the week, total your findings.** How much food did you waste during a week? How much money did it cost? Was it more or less than you thought it would be? At this rate, how much food do you waste in a year?

Try This!

How can you reduce food waste each day? Post a list of your ideas on the refrigerator so you'll be reminded not to waste food. How can your community waste less food? Find out what people are doing in your area with extra food.

Five Facts About Composting

1. The average household in the United States generates 650 pounds of compostable materials each year.

2. Composting requires only four ingredients; carbon, nitrogen, oxygen, and water. With those four ingredients, your compost pile will thrive!

3. Composting saves you money.

4. Composting lessens environmental impact, creating healthy soil for plants and trees.

5. Vermicompost is composting using worms.

BUILD A BIRD FEEDER

> **CLIMATE KIT**
> ° an empty toilet paper roll
> ° string
> ° peanut butter
> ° bird seed

Warming temperatures, shifting seasons, changing precipitation, and rising sea levels are disrupting the behavior of birds and the ecosystems that support them. In this activity, you will learn more about the birds in your area by building your very own bird feeder.

❯ Punch two holes at one end of the toilet paper roll, about 3 centimeters from the top of the roll.

❯ **Put a string through both holes.** Tie the loose ends of the string together. This will be how you hang your bird feeder.

❯ **Cover the outside of the toilet paper roll in peanut butter.**

❯ **Roll the peanut butter-covered toilet paper roll in a plate of bird seed,** making sure the seeds coat the peanut butter.

❯ **Hang your bird feeder outside.** Ideally, you will be able to see it through a window.

❯ **Get ready for a bird party!**

Try This!

Warmer temperatures are forcing birds to winter and breed farther north than in the past. Many species once found farther south, including popular birds such as northern cardinals and tufted titmice, are expanding their ranges into New England. Take your bird feeder a step further by cataloging the types of birds you are seeing and when you see them. You may need a bird book or the internet to help you identify the birds that come to your feeder.

GLOSSARY

absorb: to soak up a liquid or take in energy, heat, light, or sound.

acid: a sour substance that dissolves some minerals.

adapt: to change to survive in new or different conditions.

agriculture: growing crops and raising animals for food.

air pressure: the force of air on something.

algae: a plant-like organism that lives in water and grows by converting energy from the sun into food.

atmosphere: the mixture of gases surrounding a planet.

atmospheric pressure: the force created by the weight of the atmosphere.

avalanche: a sudden and quick downhill flow of snow and ice from a mountain.

axis: the imaginary line through the North and South Poles that the earth rotates around.

bacteria: single-celled organisms found in soil, water, plants, and animals. They help decay food and some bacteria are harmful. Singular is bacterium.

basic: describes a substance with a bitter taste that often feels slippery. Soap is usually a base. So is baking soda and ammonia.

BCE: put after a date, BCE stands for Before Common Era and counts down to zero. CE stands for Common Era and counts up from zero. This book was printed in 2020 CE.

biofuel: fuel made from living matter, such as plants.

black carbon: the sooty black material emitted from gas and diesel engines, coal-fired power plants, and other sources that burn fossil fuels.

boreal forest: a northern forest filled mostly with conifers, which are trees with needles that produce cones.

calcium: a mineral found in shells and bones.

carbon: an element found in living things, including plants. Carbon is also found in diamonds, charcoal, and graphite.

carbon cycle: the way carbon is exchanged between the atmosphere and Earth's ecosystems.

carbon dioxide (CO_2): a combination of carbon and oxygen that is formed by the burning of fossil fuels, the rotting of plants and animals, and the breathing out of animals or humans.

carbon footprint: the total amount of carbon dioxide and other greenhouse gases emitted during the full life cycle of a product or service or by a person or family in a year.

chemosynthesis: the process some organisms use to create energy from chemicals instead of the sun.

citizen science: the involvement of everyday people in scientific activities or projects.

climate: the average weather conditions of a region during a long period of time. These conditions include temperature, air pressure, humidity, precipitation, winds, sunshine, and cloudiness.

climate change: a change in global climate patterns. In the twentieth century and beyond, climate change refers to the dramatic warming of the planet caused by increased levels of carbon dioxide in the atmosphere primarily resulting from human activity.

climatologist: a scientist who studies the climate.

collaborate: to work together with other people.

compost: to recycle food scraps and vegetation and put them back in the soil.

compress: to squeeze a material very tightly.

GLOSSARY

condense: to change from a gas to a liquid.

conservationist: a person who works to preserve nature.

conserve: to save or protect something, or to use it carefully so it isn't used up.

consumption: the use of a resource.

convection current: the movement of hot air rising and cold air sinking.

coral band: a layer added each year to coral reefs.

coral bleaching: coral that turns white, indicating it is ill and dying.

coral reef: an underwater ecosystem made by coral. Coral is an organism with a hard, outer calcium carbonate skeleton.

cyanobacteria: bacteria that use photosynthesis, better known as blue-green algae.

data: facts and observations about something.

decompose: to rot or decay.

deforestation: the process through which forests are cleared to use land for other purposes.

dendrochronology: the study of tree rings.

dense: tightly packed.

diatom: a type of algae found in both water and soil.

drought: a long period of time without rain in places that usually get rain.

ecosystem: a community of living and nonliving things and their environment.

efficient: wasting as little energy as possible.

electromagnetic wave: a wave that can travel through the emptiness of space.

element: a substance whose atoms are all the same. Examples include gold, oxygen, and carbon.

elevation: the height above sea level.

elliptical: oval or egg-shaped.

emission: something sent or given off, such as smoke, gas, heat, or light.

empower: to give someone authority and power.

endangered: a plant or animal with a very low population that is at risk of disappearing entirely.

engineer: a person who uses science, math, and creativity to design and build things.

engineering: the use of science, math, and creativity to design and build things.

environment: everything in nature, living and nonliving, including plants, animals, soil, rocks, and water.

enzyme: a substance in an organism that speeds up the rate of chemical reactions.

equator: an imaginary line around the earth, halfway between the North and South Poles.

equilibrium: balance.

evaporate: to convert from a liquid to a gas.

evolve: to change or develop gradually.

extinct: when a species completely dies out.

extremophile: an organism that can survive in environments that most others cannot.

eyepiece lens: in a telescope, the lens that refocuses the light to allow you to see the object.

fission: the splitting of an atom.

food chain: a community of animals and plants where each is eaten by another higher up in the chain.

food web: a network of connected food chains.

forecast: a prediction of the weather.

GLOSSARY

fossil: the remains or traces of an ancient plant or animal left in rock.

fossil fuels: a source of energy that comes from plants and animals that lived millions of years ago. These include coal, oil, and natural gas.

fossil record: a record of information of the past that a collection of fossils can provide.

galvanize: to shock or excite someone into taking action.

geologist: a scientist who studies the history, structure, and origin of the earth.

geothermal energy: renewable heat energy that comes from the earth.

glacier: a slowly moving mass of ice and snow.

glaciologist: a scientist who studies glaciers.

global warming: an increase in the average temperature of the earth's atmosphere, enough to cause climate change.

Goldilocks planet: a planet that orbits in the habitable zone around a star.

gravity: a force that pulls objects toward each other and all objects to the earth.

greenhouse effect: a process through which energy from the sun is trapped by a planet's atmosphere, warming it.

greenhouse gas: a gas such as water vapor, carbon dioxide, or methane that traps heat in the atmosphere and contributes to climate change.

habitable: capable of supporting life.

habitable zone: the region at a distance from a star where liquid water is likely to exist.

habitat: the natural area where a plant or animal lives.

helium: a light gas often used to fill balloons. It is the most abundant element after hydrogen.

hemisphere: half of the earth. North of the equator is called the Northern Hemisphere and south of the equator is the Southern Hemisphere.

humidity: the amount of moisture in the air.

hurricane: a severe tropical storm with winds greater than 74 miles per hour.

hydrogen: a colorless gas that is the most abundant gas in the universe.

hydrokinetic: relating to the motion of fluids.

Ice Age: a period of time when ice covered a large part of Earth.

ice core: a sample of ice taken out of a glacier, used to study climate.

incinerator: a large furnace used to burn trash.

industrialization: the widespread development of manufacturing, with products made by machines in large factories.

Industrial Revolution: a period of time beginning in the late 1700s when people started using machines to make things in large factories.

industry: the large-scale production of goods, especially in factories.

infrared: an invisible type of light with a longer wavelength than visible light, which can also be felt as heat.

ingenuity: the ability to solve difficult problems creatively.

innovation: a new creation or a unique solution to a problem.

iteration: using a process that repeats itself, such as developing a game, testing it, developing it further, and testing it again.

LED: light-emitting diode, which provides very efficient lighting.

lens: a clear, curved piece of glass or plastic that is used in eyeglasses, cameras, and telescopes to make things look clearer or bigger.

GLOSSARY

limestone: a kind of rock that forms from the skeletons and shells of sea creatures. Limestone can also form through precipitation of calcium and carbonate.

litmus paper: a special paper used to test whether a substance is an acid or a base.

livestock: animals raised for food and other uses.

mass: the amount of matter in an object.

Mesozoic era: a period of time from about 252 to 66 million years ago, when dinosaurs roamed the earth.

meteorologist: a scientist who studies and forecasts climate and weather.

methane: a greenhouse gas composed of carbon and hydrogen that is colorless and odorless.

microfossil: a tiny fossil that can be seen only with a microscope.

migration: the movement of a large group of animals, such as birds, due to changes in the environment.

molecule: a group of atoms bound together to form a new substance. Examples include carbon dioxide (CO_2), one carbon atom and two oxygen atoms, and water (H_2O), two hydrogen atoms and one oxygen atom. Atoms are the smallest particles of matter.

natural disaster: a natural event, such as a fire or flood, that causes great damage.

natural resource: a material or substance such as gold, wood, and water that occurs in nature and is valuable to humans.

nomadic: moving from place to place to find food and water.

nonrenewable: resources that we can't make more of and that can be used up.

nuclear energy: energy made from the splitting of an atom.

nuclear fusion: the process of hydrogen converting to helium, which releases energy and light.

nutrients: substances in food and soil that living things need to live and grow.

objective lens: in a telescope, the lens that collects light from a distant object.

ocean acidification: the process by which the ocean absorbs CO_2 from the atmosphere, and through a series of chemical reactions, becomes more acidic.

orbit: the path of an object circling another object in space.

organic: something that is or was living, such as animals, wood, grass, and insects. Also refers to food grown naturally, without chemicals.

organism: a living thing, such as a plant or animal.

oxygen: a gas in the air that people and animals need to breathe to stay alive and which is the most plentiful element on the earth.

paleoclimatology: the study of ancient climates.

paleontologist: a scientist who studies plant and animal fossils.

parts per million (ppm): a common measurement of pollution in the air.

pedologist: a scientist who studies soil.

pH: a measure of acidity or alkalinity, on a scale from 0 (most acidic) to 14 (most basic).

photoelectric effect: the creation of an electric current after exposure to light.

photosynthesis: the process by which plants produce food, using light as energy.

photovoltaic (PV): able to produce electricity from sunlight.

phytoplankton: microscopic, drifting plants, such as algae, that live in both fresh water and salt water.

planetary scientist: a person who studies the planets and natural satellites of the solar system.

GLOSSARY

plankton: microscopic plants and animals that float or drift in great numbers in bodies of water.

pollutant: a substance that is harmful to the environment.

polyp: a small creature that lives in colonies and forms coral.

precipitation: falling moisture in the form of rain, sleet, snow, or hail.

radioactive waste: the dangerous byproduct of nuclear energy.

recyclable: something that can be recycled by shredding, squashing, pulping, or melting to use the materials to create new products.

reflect: to bounce off a surface. To redirect something that hits a surface, such as heat, light, or sound.

refracting telescope: a telescope with a lens that gathers light and forms an image of something far away.

regulate: to control or to keep steady.

renewable energy: a form of energy that doesn't get used up, including the energy of the sun and the wind.

respiratory system: the parts of the body used to breathe.

rotation: a turn all the way around.

sedimentary rock: rock formed from the compression of sediments, the remains of plants and animals, or the evaporation of seawater.

silt: particles of fine soil, rich in nutrients.

solar array: an arrangement of photovoltaic devices used to collect solar energy to use as electricity.

solar panel: a device used to capture sunlight and convert it to usable energy.

solar power: energy from the sun converted to electricity.

solar system: the collection of eight planets, their moons, and other celestial bodies that orbit the sun.

species: a group of living things that are closely related and can produce young.

speed of light: the speed at which light travels, which is 186,000 miles per second.

starch: a type of nutrient found in certain foods, such as bread, potatoes, and rice.

STEM: an acronym that stands for science, technology, engineering, and mathematics. STEAM is STEM plus art.

striation: a pattern of parallel grooves or narrow bands.

stromatolite: a type of blue-green algae that uses photosynthesis to make its own food.

sunspot: a dark area on the sun's surface that is cooler than the surrounding area.

technology: the tools, methods, and systems used to solve a problem or do work.

tree ring: a layer of wood added inside a tree each year as it grows.

urban farming: growing or producing food in a city or heavily populated area.

vacuum: a space in which there is no air.

vertical farming: growing food on vertical surfaces, such as the sides of buildings or skyscrapers.

volt: the unit used to measure the electric potential between two spots in a circuit.

water cycle: the continuous movement of water from the earth to the clouds and back to the earth again.

water vapor: the gas form of water.

wavelength: the distance from crest to crest in a series of waves.

weather: the temperature, rain, and wind conditions of an area, which change daily.

wind farm: groups or clusters of wind turbines that produce large amounts of electricity together.

wind turbine: an engine fitted with blades that are spun around by the wind to generate electricity.

RESOURCES

Metric Conversions

Use this chart to find the metric equivalents to the English measurements in this book. If you need to know a half measurement, divide by two. If you need to know twice the measurement, multiply by two. How do you find a quarter measurement? How do you find three times the measurement?

English	Metric
1 inch	2.5 centimeters
1 foot	30.5 centimeters
1 yard	0.9 meter
1 mile	1.6 kilometers
1 pound	0.5 kilogram
1 teaspoon	5 milliliters
1 tablespoon	15 milliliters
1 cup	237 milliliters

WEBSITES FOR KIDS

US Energy Information Administration: *eia.gov/kids*

NOAA for Kids: *oceanservice.noaa.gov/kids*

NASA's Climate Kids: *climatekids.nasa.gov/nasa-research*

National Geographic Kids Climate Change: *kids.nationalgeographic.com/explore/science/climate-change*

WEBSITES FOR EDUCATORS

Energy Information Administration for Teachers: *eia.gov/kids/energy.php?page=6*

NASA Greenhouse Gases (Cards): *climatekids.nasa.gov/greenhouse-cards*

Teacher-Friendly Guides to Earth Science of the United States: *geology.teacherfriendlyguide.org*

Explore the Critical Zone: *youtube.com/watch?v=8gW-Vy7zFdU*

Will Steger Foundation Climate Lessons: *willstegerfoundation.org/climate-lessons-blog*

NEED (National Energy Education Development) Project: *need.org*

Climate Literacy & Energy Awareness Network (CLEAN): *cleanet.orgNOAA*

Teaching Climate: *climate.gov/teachingClimate Change Educationncse.com/climate*

TED-Ed—A Guide to the Energy of the Earth: *ed.ted.com/lessons/a-guide-to-the-energy-of-the-earth-joshua-m-sneideman*

Energy Videos from the International Museum Network: *sciencebeyondtheboundaries.com/EnergyVideos.htm*

RESOURCES

ESSENTIAL QUESTIONS

Introduction: Why is it important to track data for long periods of time instead of short periods of time?

Chapter 1: How do scientists know if a planet is a Goldilocks planet? What do they measure to find out?

Chapter 2: How does the sun affect Earth? Could we have life without the sun?

Chapter 3: Why are the carbon cycle and water cycle important to Earth's climate? What happens when they get disrupted?

Chapter 4: How do scientists learn about Earth's climate as it was billions of years ago?

Chapter 5: How is human activity warming the planet?

Chapter 6: How can we help support the health of planet Earth?

QR CODE GLOSSARY

Page 6: youtube.com/watch?v=Z43FQCSg4Ow

Page 9: scied.ucar.edu/dog-walking-weather-and-climate

Page 13: jpl.nasa.gov/video/details.php?id=900

Page 18: youtube.com/watch?v=1Ll-VHYxWXU

Page 30: ptaff.ca/soleil/?lang=en_CA

Page 32: nca2014.globalchange.gov/highlights/report-findings/extreme-weather

Page 35: energy.gov/maps/how-does-wind-turbine-work

Page 43: climatekids.nasa.gov/greenhouse-cards

Page 52: youtube.com/watch?v=o_bbQ0m3wuM

Page 53: mars.jpl.nasa.gov/msl/multimedia/videos/index.cfm?v=49;space.com/27217-nasa-mars-maven-spacecraft-arrival.html

Page 59: youtube.com/watch?v=V0d7DcPsuZU

Page 61: youtu.be/VbSzoebC-8o

Page 62: coral.bios.edu/prism

Page 64: youtube.com/watch?v=I_dC2swK9AY

Page 67: dataintheclassroom.noaa.gov/?utm_medium=email&utm_source=GovDelivery

Page 75: climate.nasa.gov/climate_resources/139/graphic-global-warming-from-1880-to-2018

Page 80: www3.epa.gov/carbon-footprint-calculator

Page 94: youtube.com/watch?v=ir4XngHcohM

Page 96: acespace.org

Page 97: climatemuseum.org

Page 104: youngvoicesfortheplanet.com/youth-climate-videos/green-ambassadors

Page 108: pbskids.org/scigirls

INDEX

A

activities
  Build a Bird Feeder, 113
  Build a Solar Cooker, 22–23
  Build Your Own Anemometer, 41
  Build Your Own Sundial, 37
  Can Crusher, 19
  Carbon in the Air, 89
  Core Sampling, 71
  Decomposition Experiment, 55
  Experiment with Dry Ice, 53
  Explore the Planets, 20
  Fossil Collection, 69
  How Powerful is Sunlight?, 40
  Investigate Weather, 9
  Light Over Time, 88
  Make an Apple Battery, 38–39
  Make a Telescope, 21
  Measure Air Pollutants, 86
  Measure the Moisture in the Air, 54
  Ocean Acidification, 72–73
  Perform a Transportation Energy Audit, 87
  Plant Trees in Your Community, 109
  Soil Scientist, 70
  Track Your Waste, 112
  Write a Letter to the Mayor or the Governor, 110–111
Alley, Richard, 61
animals, 2, 3, 24–26, 36, 45–47, 60–66, 78–79, 84, 106, 113
atmosphere
  air/atmospheric pressure in, 19, 35
  gases in, 5, 7, 13–15, 26, 42–55, 58–59, 68, 76–78, 80–83, 85, 87, 89, 101–102, 109. *See also* specific gases
  Goldilocks planets's, 10–19
  heat trapped by, 5, 13–15, 18, 25–26, 45

B

Black, Joseph, iv, 49

C

carbon cycle, 49
carbon dioxide
  atmospheric balance of, 5, 7, 44–45, 47–49, 68, 101–102, 109
  carbon footprint of, 80, 87, 101, 105
  discovery of, iv, 49
  fossil fuel burning creating, 3–4, 5, 15, 68, 73, 77, 81–82, 87, 89
  frozen, 53
  heat trapped by, 5, 13–15, 45
  historical study of, iv–v, 59, 63, 77
  measurement of, iv–v, 6, 77, 80
  reduction of, 85, 92, 101–103, 105
careers/"green jobs," 104
climate
  definition of, 2, 9, 31
  Goldilocks planets, 10–18. *See also* Earth; Mars; Venus
  historical study of, iv–v, 56–73
  sun's role in. *See* sun
  temperature; temperature
  weather and, 2, 9, 31–32
climate change
  definition of, 2
  environmental protection from, iv–v, 7–8, 76, 77, 84–85, 92–113
  extreme weather and, 2, 32
  fossil fuel burning role in, iv, 2, 3–4, 5, 15, 26, 43–45, 68, 73, 76–78, 81–85, 87, 89
  global warming and, 26, 63, 74–85, 95

greenhouse gases
  contributing to, 5, 14–15, 26, 42–55, 58–59, 68, 76–78, 80–83, 85, 87, 89. *See also* specific gases
  history of, iv–v, 56–73
  human activity affecting, 3–5, 15, 26, 42–45, 75–85, 90–92
  measurement of, 5–7
composting, 102, 105, 107, 112
coral reefs, 56, 60–64

D

dendrochronology, 66–67

E

Earth
  atmosphere of. *See* atmosphere
  global warming, 26, 63, 74–85, 95. *See also* climate change
  as Goldilocks planet, 10–12, 14–15, 18
  photographs of, 3, 18
  as spaceship, 1–2
  sun's effects on. *See* sun
  water on. *See* water
Einstein, Albert, 35
energy. *See* fossil fuels; renewable energy; sun
environmental protection, iv–v, 7–8, 76, 77, 84–85, 92–113
extreme conditions, 2, 13, 31, 32

F

food and farming, 3, 4, 5, 22, 24–26, 36, 48, 78–80, 83, 90, 99–102, 105, 112
Foote, Eunice, iv, 5
fossil fuels, iv, 2, 3–4, 5, 15, 26, 43–45, 68, 73, 76–78, 81–85, 87, 89
fossils, 56, 65, 67–69

INDEX

G

global warming, 26, 63, 74–85, 95. *See also* climate change
Goldilocks planets, 10–18. *See also* Earth; Mars; Venus
greenhouse effect, 14–15
greenhouse gases, 5, 14–15, 26, 42–55, 58–59, 68, 76–78, 80–83, 85, 87, 89. *See also* specific gases

H

humans
    contributions to climate change, 3–5, 15, 26, 42–45, 75–85, 90–92
    digestion and gases in, 43–44
    environmental protection by, iv–v, 7–8, 76, 77, 84–85, 92–113
    population of, v, 3, 80–81
    respiration and carbon dioxide in, 47
    temperature regulation in, 52

I

ice and glaciers, v, 11, 18, 32, 51, 53, 56–61, 67, 81
Industrial Revolution, 58, 90–91

K

Keeling, Charles David/Keeling Curve, 5, 6
Kepler, Johannes/Kepler Space Telescope, 11

M

Mars, 12, 15–18, 19, 53
Mead, Margaret, 108
methane, 15, 44–47, 55, 78, 85
Moms Clean Air Force, 85

N

nitrogen, 5, 7

O

Obama, Barack, 92
oceans, 11, 26, 44, 49–52, 60–66, 72–73, 94, 102–103
oxygen, iv, 5, 7, 47, 49–50, 67–68, 101, 109

P

Paris Agreement, v, 77
Priestley, Joseph, iv, 49

R

rain, 2, 31–32, 35, 52
Raymond, Eleanor, 33
recycling, 38, 102, 105
renewable energy, iv–v, 26, 32–36, 40–41, 81–82, 85, 92, 93–95, 98, 102. *See also* under sun

S

Sagan, Carl, 15
seasons, 2, 29–31, 32
sun
    atmosphere trapping heat from, 5, 13–15, 18, 25–26, 45
    definition and description of, 27–28
    energy/solar power from, iv–v, 2, 22–28, 32–36, 40, 44–45, 51–52, 93–94, 98, 102
    Goldilocks planets's distance from, 12, 13, 17
    planets orbiting, 11, 30
    seasons and, 29–31, 32
    sunspots on, 28
    weather affected by, 31–32

T

Telkes, Mária, 33
temperature
    atmosphere trapping heat and raising, 5, 13–15, 18, 25–26, 45
    extreme, 31
    Goldilocks planets's, 10–18
    historical study of, iv–v, 56–73
    recording of, 75
    rising. *See* climate change; global warming
    sun's role in, 12–15, 17–18, 25–32, 35, 45
    urban heat islands, 100
    water cycle regulating, 51–52
Thunberg, Greta, v, 95–96
transportation, iv, 3–4, 22, 45, 82, 84, 87, 98
trees and forests, 3, 5, 47–49, 66–67, 82–83, 100–101, 103, 105, 109

V

Venus, 13–15, 17, 19

W

Washington, Warren, 83
waste/trash disposal, 3, 36, 38, 46–47, 55, 102–103, 112
water
    carbon dioxide in, 49–51, 63, 73, 102
    consumption of, 3, 79, 105
    energy/hydropower from, iv, 35, 82, 94
    frozen, v, 11, 18, 32, 35, 51, 53, 56–61, 67, 81
    Goldilocks planets's, 11, 13, 15, 18
    ocean, 11, 26, 44, 49–52, 60–66, 72–73, 94, 102–103
    rain, 2, 31–32, 35, 52
    water cycle, 2, 15, 35, 51–52
    water vapor, 7, 11, 13, 15, 44, 51–52, 54
weather/weather patterns, 2, 9, 31–32
wind/wind power, v, 2, 35, 41, 82, 93